The Renaissance and the Celtic Countries

T0366548

Note from the Series Editor

This volume marks the second publication in the occasional series of essay collections published for the Society for Renaissance Studies by Blackwell Publishing. These collections make available in book form selected special numbers of the Society's journal, *Renaissance Studies*. The volumes are all guest edited, and all the material appearing will also have been peer-reviewed in the normal way, and approved by the journal's editorial board.

John E. Law,
Series Editor

The editors of this special number of *Renaissance Studies* are grateful for the support of the Society for Renaissance Studies and the department of History, Classics and Ancient History, and Welsh at the University of Wales, Swansea.

Previous books in the series:
Daniel Carey, Editor, *Asian Travel in the Renaissance* (2004)

The Renaissance and the Celtic Countries

Edited by
Ceri Davies and John E. Law

**Published on behalf of the
Society for Renaissance Studies**

© 2005 by the Society for Renaissance Studies, Blackwell Publishing Ltd

First published as a special issue of *Renaissance Studies*

BLACKWELL PUBLISHING
350 Main Street, Malden, MA 02148-5020, USA
108 Cowley Road, Oxford OX4 1JF, UK
550 Swanston Street, Carlton, Victoria 3053, Australia

The right of Ceri Davies and John E. Law to be identified as the Authors of the Editorial
Material in this Work has been asserted in accordance with the UK Copyright, Designs, and
Patents Act 1988.

First published 2005 by Blackwell Publishing Ltd

Library of Congress Cataloging-in-Publication Data has been applied for

ISBN 1-4051-2063-0

A catalogue record for this title is available from the British Library.

Set in 10/12pt New Baskerville by Graphicraft Limited, Hong Kong
Printed and bound in the United Kingdom
by MPG Books Ltd, Bodmin, Cornwall

The publisher's policy is to use permanent paper from mills that operate a sustainable forestry
policy, and which has been manufactured from pulp processed using acid-free and elementary
chlorine-free practices. Furthermore, the publisher ensures that the text paper and cover board
used have met acceptable environmental accreditation standards.

For further information on
Blackwell Publishing, visit our website:
www.blackwellpublishing.com

Contents

Preface

The five essays included in this volume of *Renaissance Studies* were first presented at a one-day conference, entitled 'The Renaissance and the Celtic Countries', held at the University of Wales, Swansea, on 20 October 2001. The conference was arranged under the joint auspices of the University and the Society for Renaissance Studies, and it is a pleasurable duty to thank both bodies for their support. A special word of gratitude is due to the five guest speakers, both for their contributions on the day and for preparing their papers for publication.

Fourteen years earlier, in July 1987, the International Congress of Celtic Studies met in Swansea for its quadrennial conference and took the Celts and the Renaissance as its central theme. The papers of that highly successful meeting were published as Glanmor Williams and Robert Owen Jones (eds), *The Celts and the Renaissance: Tradition and Innovation* (Cardiff, 1990). In the intervening period some of the countries of the 'Celtic fringe' have undergone far-reaching changes, notably in the wake of political devolution in Scotland and Wales. It was therefore both appropriate and timely that Swansea should again play host to a meeting devoted to considering aspects of the Renaissance in the experience of some of the writers and scholars of Ireland, Scotland, and Wales.

The coupling of the words 'Celtic' and 'Renaissance' may, at first sight, come as a little surprising. Celtic elements have often been viewed as forces which were bent on shackling native cultures to their past and resisting any Renaissance-inspired influences. The problem was famously addressed by David Mathew in his pioneering work, *The Celtic Peoples and Renaissance Europe* (London, 1933), and succinctly summarized by Christopher Dawson in his introduction to that book:

> there was no room for . . . compromise between the ancient Celtic society and the new Renaissance state. No sociological contact was possible between the Tudor courtier with his mind attuned to all the subtleties of political intrigue and to all the refinements of Renaissance culture, and the Gaelic chieftain who still reckoned his wealth in cattle and his renown by the praises of his hereditary bards.

The papers presented at the 1987 Celtic Congress did much to dispel this image of an unbridgeable gap between Celtic societies and the Renaissance world, and demonstrated that in the Gaelic literatures of Ireland and Scotland, and especially the Welsh-language literature of Wales, there was ample evidence of the impact of Renaissance humanism on native cultures. The focus of three of the studies contained in the present collection is on aspects of the work of some of the most notable of the Latin humanist writers who emerged from Ireland, Scotland, and Wales, while another discusses the role – within Scottish society – of the greatest of the instruments of the Renaissance, the printed book. The fifth paper, however, is an apt reminder that tension between the upholding of traditional expectations and the espousal of classically inspired humanism was not easily resolved and could still lead to a sense of ideological confrontation.

Ceri Davies

1

Richard Stanihurst's De Rebus in Hibernia Gestis[1]

John Barry

The object of this paper is to examine certain aspects of *De Rebus* in order to show what light it casts on Stanihurst, his country, and his community. By way of introduction, I shall sketch briefly the circumstances under which *De Rebus* was written, and after that read the text with reference to two headings, Stanihurst the scholar and Stanihurst the Palesman.

THE GENESIS OF DE REBUS

Richard Stanihurst was born in 1547 to a well-to-do family of Dublin Palesmen. His great grandfather, also called Richard, was lord mayor of Dublin in 1489. His grandfather, Nicholas, was involved in administration and, although the Stanihursts were Catholic, was well placed to extend the family landholdings after the dissolution of the monasteries in 1542. Stanihurst's father, James, was speaker of the Irish House of Commons on three occasions. He presided over the restoration of papal supremacy under Queen Mary in 1557 and over the dissolution of the same reforms under Elizabeth in 1560, displaying a loyalty and obedience to the British crown which is one of the themes of *De Rebus*.[2] As a matter of policy towards civilizing the native Irish, James Stanihurst hoped to see the spread of grammar school education in Ireland 'whereby good learning is supported, and our unquiet neighbours would find such sweetness in the taste thereof as it should be a ready way to reclaim them.'[3]

One such grammar school was that of Peter White in Kilkenny, and here Richard Stanihurst was sent in 1557. White was a graduate of Oriel College, Oxford and the author of a textbook *Epitomae Copiae Erasmi*,[4] as well as of works on rhetoric, on two speeches of Cicero, and on Latin epigrams.[5] Stanihurst

---

[1] Published by Christopher Plantin (Antwerp, 1584). Hereafter referred to as *De Rebus*.

[2] Details of the history of Richard Stanihurst and his family are largely drawn from Dr Colm Lennon's excellent biography *Richard Stanihurst the Dubliner* (Dublin, 1981). I have also had a preview of Dr Lennon's forthcoming article, 'Richard Stanihurst (and his family)', for the *New Dictionary of National Biography*. My thanks to him.

[3] James Stanihurst's words in Edmund Campion, *Two Bokes of the Histories of Ireland*, ed. A. F. Vossen (Assen, 1963), 181.

[4] Anthony Wood, *Athenae Oxonienses*, ed. P. Bliss (London, 1813–20), II, 252.

[5] Lennon, *Richard Stanihurst*, 25; see also W. B. Stanford, *Ireland and the Classical Tradition* (Dublin, 1984), 19.

received a sound education with a classical humanist base and, as will be seen later, a solid grounding in Ciceronian *imitatio.*

In 1563 Stanihurst went up to Oxford, to University College, from where he graduated B.A. in 1568. During his time there he became a protégé and friend of Edmund Campion. Campion encouraged him to write and later to publish a work on the third-century Greek Neoplatonist, Porphyry. The work, entitled *Harmonia, seu catena dialectica in Porphyrianas institutiones,* was completed in 1556 (published by Reginald Wolf, London, 1570) and dedicated to Sir Henry Sidney, who became a patron of the Stanihurst family.[6]

After graduation from Oxford, Richard Stanihurst went on to study law at Furnival's and Lincoln's Inns in London. In 1570 he returned to Ireland, accompanied by Edmund Campion, who was becoming increasingly dissatisfied with the Protestantism which was permeating intellectual life in Oxford. Campion found the Stanihurst household an ideal retreat, with good company and a well-stocked library, of manuscripts and documents as well as books, and began work on a history of Ireland.[7]

But the political climate was changing: in 1571 Sir Henry Sidney sent warning that Campion would be arrested if found; Sidney himself was being recalled to London. With the connivance of the Stanihursts, Campion hid out for ten weeks at the house of Sir Christopher Barnewall in Drogheda, before returning to England and moving from there to the continent. During these ten weeks he wrote his *Two Bokes of the Histories of Ireland.* He left a copy with Richard Stanihurst, who later 'fully resolved to enrich Master Campion's chronicle with further additions'.[8] This was the basis of Stanihurst's contribution to Holinshed's *Chronicles* and later of his *De Rebus.*

The withdrawal of Sidney meant the loss of a powerful patron to the Stanihursts. Also, power was being taken out of the hands of the Dublin-based nobility (Palesmen) and given to staunch Protestants, who were sent from London. James Stanihurst was replaced by John Crofton, newly arrived from London.[9] No Stanihurst after held high office, and from 1575 to 1580 Richard was in London in the post of tutor to Garret FitzGerald, the son of the Earl of Kildare. In 1577 his contribution 'A plain and perfect Description of Ireland' appeared in Holinshed's *Chronicles.*

He left England in 1581, after the execution of Campion, and went to the Spanish Netherlands. In Leiden, in 1582, he published a translation into

---

[6] Lennon, *Richard Stanihurst,* 26. There is a good account of the *Harmonia* in Lennon's forthcoming *New DNB* article (cf. note 2).

[7] Edmund Campion, *Opuscula Omnia,* ed. R. Turner (Cologne, 1625), 208: 'you set me up with a library selected from your own and you provided so admirably that I should have ease and opportunity for study, that may I perish if I ever conversed so sweetly with the muses outside of Oxford's walls'. Cited by Lennon, *Richard Stanihurst,* 28.

[8] Lennon, *Richard Stanihurst,* 33, quoting from R. Holinshed (ed.), *Chronicles of England, Scotland and Ireland* (London, 1577), III, A1ʳ–A1ᵛ.

[9] Cf. Lennon, *Richard Stanihurst,* 34.

(the first) English hexameters of the first four books of the *Aeneid*,[10] and in 1584 came *De Rebus*.

STANIHURST THE SCHOLAR

Stanihurst was educated by the pedagogical method, common in the Renaissance,[11] of *imitatio*: the use of classical models for contemporary purposes. This had an immense influence on content, vocabulary, and style.

De Rebus is an account, in four books, of the Norman conquest of Ireland. The first book is ethnographical; books two, three, and four are narrative. The work is prefaced by a dedicatory letter to Stanihurst's brother-in-law Patrick Plunkett, Baron Dunsany. At the end of the letter Stanihurst says 'it will be of great use to my project to set down some things pertaining to the situation of the land the nature of the island and the character of the inhabitants. Truly I perceive that such a prelude has found favour with the greatest historians.'[12]

By this statement, Stanihurst places himself in the tradition of classical ethnography, a subgenre of classical literature, whether scientific, philosophical, epic, or lyric, from earliest times, respected and used by 'the greatest historians', the models which Stanihurst followed: Sallust, Caesar, Livy, Tacitus.

The great German scholar Eduard Norden collected instances of the phrase 'de situ +genitive' to prove that it was the standard title for Latin ethnographical works.[13] A brief account of this tradition will help to show its influence on the content of *De Rebus*: the use of the technical vocabulary and the methodology of classical ethnography.

The tradition begins with Homer. In the *Odyssey* especially, we note the interest in the description of the geographical position and the nature of various lands, and the characteristics of the inhabitants – nough to mention the Cyclopes (*Odyssey* 9.105–40). In the sixth century BC colonization led to an increased interest in scientific methodology. Fragments of Hecataeus of Miletus represent a body of work with titles like *periodos* (travel book) or *periegesis* (sketch).[14]

The artistic potential of the form was developed by Herodotus in the fifth century BC, and the true practical value of the genre was realized in the writings of the Hippocratic school: environment affects the health and

[10] Richard Stanihurst, *The First Four Books of Virgil's Aeneis Translated into English Heroical Verse* (Leyden, 1582). A more recent edition is Dirk Van der Haar, *Richard Stanyhurst's Aeneis* (Amsterdam, 1933).

[11] And earlier: see R. R. Bolgar, *The Classical Heritage and its Beneficiaries* (Cambridge, 1997), 23–4, 'the habit of reading, notebook in hand to collect telling words and phrases, metaphors, parts of speech and arguments, and the desirability of memorising this material until it became part of the natural furnishing of one's mind'.

[12] '. . . quae ad terrae situm, insulae naturam, incolarum mores pertinent . . .', *De Rebus* 14.

[13] E. Norden, *Die Germanische Urgeschichte in Tacitus Germania* (Berlin, 1920), I, 451–4. Cf. R. F. Thomas, *Lands and People in Roman Poetry: The Ethnographical tradition* (Cambridge, 1982), 3: 'The phrase, then, acts as an ethnographical *sphragis*.'

[14] G. Nenci, *Hecataei Milesii Fragmenta* (Florence, 1954).

ultimately the character of the inhabitants.[15] In the following century, the
Peripatetic school added to the methodology the description of the origins,
settlement, migration, and historical relations of peoples. Throughout the
genre there runs an interest in strange and wonderful things (*thaumasia*).

The transmission of this material from Greek to Roman writers is mainly
the work of the Stoic philosopher Posidonius (135–51 BC), whose school at
Rhodes was a Mecca for Roman intellectuals, among them Cicero.

We may summarize this sketchy outline of the development of classical
ethnography with a schema of the elements it comprises:

1. Physical geography of a region: situation, boundaries, size, mountains,
   rivers, harbours, etc.
2. Origins and features of the inhabitants.
3. Climate, defined in relation to an ideal of temperateness (*caeli temperatio*).
4. Agricultural produce (crops trees and stock); mineral resources.
5. Political, social and military organization.
6. A moralizing view of this material.[16]

How well Stanihurst appropriated classical methodology may be seen from
the fact that most of the material in the first book of *De Rebus* can be classified
under the above headings. A brief excerpt will serve to illustrate. In the dedicatory epistle mentioned above, Stanihurst laments the fact that, while the most
remote parts of the world are becoming daily better known, Ireland remains
completely ignored by scholars (except for Ortelius, of whom more anon):

> Neque enim huiusce rei culpa in florentissimam insulam est conferenda,
> cum qua quidem caeli salubritate, agrorum fertilitate, ubertate frugum,
> amoenitate fontium, opportunitate fluvium, portuosis stationibus,
> silvarum proceritate, ditissimis metallorum venis, pastionis magnitudine,
> armentorum gregibus conferre paucas, anteferre nullas regiones valeas.
> Quod si in huius insulae incolas oculos inferre velis, illi quidem corporis
> commoditate, ingenii acumine, ceterisque animi ornamentis usque eo
> praestant, ut nihil eis aut natura non oblatum, aut ab industria recusatum
> videatur. (*De Rebus* 4)

[Blame for this cannot be laid on that most flourishing island. Indeed for
healthiness of climate, fertility of land, abundance of crops, pleasantness
of springs, usefulness of rivers, number of safe anchorages, height of
timber, richness of veins of metals, expanse of pasture, flocks and herds,
you can find few regions to compare, none to prefer. And if you wish to

---

[15] J. J. Tierney, 'The Celtic ethnography of Posidonius', *Proceedings of the Royal Irish Academy*, 60/C (1960), 190.
[16] In this outline I have followed R. M. Ogilvie and I. Richmond (eds), *Cornelii Taciti De Vita Agricolae* (Oxford, 1978), 164. I have added item 6.

consider the inhabitants of this island, they are so excellent in shapeliness
of body, sharpness of intellect and other ornaments of the mind that there
seems to be nothing that nature has not presented to them or they have
not achieved by their own efforts.]

Remember that this is only in the introduction, not in the narrative proper.
It is a proleptic passage: Stanihurst is, if you like, making headings, and it is
notable that the headings coincide remarkably with items one to four of the
list above. The author's methodology owes much to the process of *imitatio*.

Posidonius was an important geographer and ethnographer, but he was
primarily a Stoic philosopher and introduced elements of Stoicism into the
tradition of ethnography.[17] In this regard, when he described the way of life
of barbarians on the fringes of the empire, he did so with Stoic coloration:
the barbarian despises luxury; dresses, eats, and dwells simply; has the qualities of *duritia* (hardiness, austerity) and *patientia* (endurance). In short, he
is a model of the ethical behaviour to which the Roman Stoic aspires. We can
trace this tradition through Cicero to Stanihurst and see how ethnography
provides the philosopher with material for a moral lecture.

Cicero takes the example of Anacharsis the Scythian:

An Scythes Anacharsis potuit pro nihilo pecuniam ducere, nostrates
philosophi non poterunt? . . . mihi amictui est Scythicum tegimen, calcia-
mentum solorum callum, cubile terra, pulpamentum fames, lacte caseo,
carne vescor   (*Tusculan Disputations* 5.32)

[Could the Scythian Anacharsis disregard money and shall not our
philosophers not be able to do so? . . . 'my clothing is the same as that
with which the Scythians cover themselves; the hardness of my feet supplies the want of shoes; the ground is my bed, hunger my sauce, my food
milk, cheese and flesh'.[18]]

Compare Stanihurst:

Bellicosus quidem ille miles et nervosus haberi debet, qui sudo et udo
caelo aptus est, qui ad omnes labores impiger invenitur, qui famem pro
condimento; nasturtium pro cibo, humum pro cubili, arbustum pro
tabernaculo habet   (*De Rebus* 52)

[That soldier must indeed be considered warlike and tough who is prepared for clear sky or wet, who is found keen in the face of every hardship,

[17] R. F. Thomas, *Lands and Peoples*, 2.

[18] Translation by C. D. Yonge, *The Academic Questions, Treatise De Finibus and Tusculan Disputations of M. T. Cicero* (London, 1853), 463.

who has hunger for sauce, cress for food, the ground for a bed, the wood for a tent.]

It is clear that the ethnographical tradition provides the Stoic topos, and Cicero provides the model of style and vocabulary for Stanihurst's *imitatio*. The classical topos, however, serves a contemporary purpose. The passage quoted just now comes from the end of book one of *De Rebus*, where Stanihurst is concerned to dispel the myth that the Irish live like wild animals, wandering in the woods and 'eating hay like cattle'.[19] The myth arose, according to Stanihurst, because of the conditions endured by some outlaws who lived wild in the woods (although he says, 'they are rarely found, even in their caves without sauces and wine'[20]). The moral lecture is developed: robbery is, of course, not to be condoned, but the toughness (*duritia*) has in it something laudable; it produces good soldiers. The sermon is enhanced by two witty passages. One is a pen-picture of an effete modern soldier:

Quem enim potes mollem et enervatum novitium aliquo in numero putare, qui cum hoste non valet confligere, nisi dulcicula potione et quibusdam sportellis sustentetur, imo nisi, abdomini natus, crapulam cottidie exhalet, nisi unguentorum odore nares recreet, nisi sub pellibus interquiescat, nisi variis vestibus et nescio quibus lacernis oneretur?   (*De Rebus* 52)

[What soft and effeminate novice can you consider to be of any account, who cannot fight the enemy unless he is sustained by a sweet little drink and some treats, or rather, since he is born the slave of his belly, unless he sleeps off a hangover each day; unless he refreshes his nose with the scent of perfume; unless he rests between times under fur coverlets; unless he is laden with all sorts of clothing and mantles?[21]]

The second colouring passage is a story about a pair of robbers who had kept vigil all night in bitter cold weather. They were settling down to sleep in the

---

[19] 'Faenumque, instar pecudum, esse', *De Rebus* 51.

[20] 'Tametsi raro, absque obsoniis et vino, etiam in suis cavernis, inveniantur', *De Rebus* 51.

[21] This must have been a common topos in Stanihurst's time. Compare Hotspur's speech in Henry the Fourth, Part 1, Act I, sc. iii, which plays on the contrast between the tough warrior and the effeminate courtier:

> My liege, I did deny no prisoners,
> But I remember when the fight was done,
> When I was dry with rage and extreme toil,
> Breathless and faint, leaning upon my sword,
> Came there a certain lord, neat, trimly dress'd,
> Fresh as a bridegroom; and his chin new reaped
> Showed like a stubble land at harvest home;
> He was perfumed like a milliner;
> And 'twixt his finger and his thumb he held
> A pouncet box, which ever and anon
> He gave to his nose, and took't away again.

snow, and one of them rolled a snowball to put under his head, 'but the other, vexed at the softness of his comrade, is reported to have said, "surely you ought to be whipped, you cowardly and effeminate recruit. I ask you, are you so flushed with softness that you cannot, out of a night's tiredness, sleep without a pillow?" '[22]

As a scholar, Stanihurst also displays an awareness of the work of other scholars of his period. The interest in ethnography, which we have just considered, serves also to mark Stanihurst's place in one of the great areas of Renaissance study. Stanihurst had, as we have seen, contributed a description of Ireland to Holinshed's *Chronicles* (above, 1). He was also a correspondent of Ortelius, the producer of the famous *Theatrum Orbis Terrarum*.[23] Another correspondent of Ortelius was the great Welsh scholar Humphrey Llwyd. Stanihurst refers to a letter and a description of Britain by Llwyd written to Ortelius[24] in which Llwyd, following Juvenal,[25] approves of *Iuverna* as the origin of the name *Hibernia*. 'But,' says Stanihurst, 'even though I grant to this glutton for antiquity as much respect as I think is due to a man so learned and erudite, yet in this I cannot but disagree with his opinion.'[26] According to Stanihurst, following 'our Annals',[27] the name derives either from *Hiberus* (the river Ebro) or Iberus, the second king of the Spanish, from whom the Irish are sprung. As added authority he cites the Spanish scholar Franciscus Tarrafa.[28]

Stanihurst then goes on to deal with the ambiguity of the names *Scotia* and *Scotti*, which brings him to the origin legend of Gaidelus, the Greek mercenary, and Scota, the Pharaoh's daughter. When Gaedelus came to Ireland his Greek followers called themselves Scotti and the island Scotia, in honour of the lady. Stanihurst gives Hector Boece[29] as an authority for this, noting that Llwyd, and after him George Buchanan,[30] reject the theory as an 'empty fable of a poetess'.[31] He does not give an opinion on the veracity or falsehood of the legend, but sides with Buchanan in a scathing criticism of Boece which culminates with 'while to lie on purpose is a disgrace in all circumstances, in history it is most disgraceful'.[32]

---

[22] 'Alter, contubernalis sui mollitiem aegre ferens, dixisse fertur, Nae tu quidem(excors ac effaeminate tiro) vapulare debes. Tantane, amabo te, mollitia fluis, ut non absque pulvinari, ex nocturna lassitudine, dormire valeas?' *De Rebus* 53.

[23] Abraham Ortelius, *Theatrum Orbis Terrarum* (Antwerp, 1570).

[24] In 1568. Llwyd's work was the *Commentarioli Britannicae Descriptionis Fragmentum*, published by Ortelius in 1572. Stanihurst, however, cites it (*De Rebus* 16, marginale) under the title *Breviarium Britanniae*. Possibly he was working from an English translation by Thomas Twyne, *The Breviary of Britayne* (London, 1573). See C. Davies, *Latin Writers of the Renaissance* (Cardiff, 1981), 21–2.

[25] *Satire* 2, 159–60.

[26] 'Verum licet tantum huic vetustatis heluoni tribuam, quantum docto et erudito viro tribuendum censeam, in hoc tamen ab illius sententia non queo non discrepare', *De Rebus* 16.

[27] 'Vetus igitur, et vera opinio nostrorum Annalium est . . .', *De Rebus* 16.

[28] Franciscus Tarrafa, *De Origine et rebus gestis Regum Hispaniae Liber* (Antwerp, 1553).

[29] Hector Boethius (= Boece), *Scotorum Historiae* (Paris, 1526).

[30] Stanihurst cites Humphrey Llwyd, *Breviarium Britanniae* and George Buchanan, *Rerum Scotticarum Historia* (Antwerp, 1583).

[31] 'Vanam poetriae fabella', *De Rebus* 16.

[32] *De Rebus* 19.

Much work needs to be done on the range of references to other scholars in *De Rebus*. For the purposes of this paper, I think enough has been said to demonstrate the liveliness and depth of Stanihurst's scholarship. He was truly a fitting member of the *res publica litterarum*.

We now turn to a consideration of the lexis or, as Stanihurst would have put it, the *elocutio*[33] of the *De Rebus*. By analysing two passages, I hope to show that his training in *imitatio* for the most part served him well, but sometimes led him astray.

In the third book of *De Rebus* there is a description of Raymond FitzGerald, one of the leaders of the Norman conquest of Ireland in 1169:

> Fuit Reimundus Giraldus vir longae et procerae staturae; multum cincinnatus; caesis et eminentibus oculis praeditus: nasum habuit incurvatum, et leviter a medio inflexum: vultus erat familiaris, et ut plurimum idem.   (*De Rebus* 160)

> [Raymond FitzGerald was a man long and tall in stature; had very curly hair; was endowed with prominent blue-grey eyes; he had a hooked nose, bent slightly sideways; his face was friendly and for the most part unchanging.]

In this, Stanihurst is following, fairly closely, the principal source for his history, the *Expugnatio Hibernica* of Giraldus Cambrensis.[34] Giraldus's description of Raymond is as follows:

> Erat itaque Reimundus vir ample quantitatis statureque paulo plus quam mediocris, capillis flavis et subcrispis, oculis grossis et rotundis, naso mediocriter elato, vultu colorato, hilari ac sereno . . .   (*Expugnatio* 152)

> [Raymond was a man of ample proportions, a little taller than average, with flaxen, slightly curly hair, great round eyes, a rather prominent nose, a high complexion, and a cheerful and composed expression.]

Both Giraldus and Stanihurst were imitating the author of *Ad Herennium*, where he describes a figure of thought which he calls 'portrayal' (*effictio*):

> Effictio est cum exprimitur atque effingitur verbis corporis cuiuspiam forma quoad satis sit ad intellegendum, hoc modo: 'Hunc, iudices, dico, rubrum, brevem, incurvum, canum, subcrispum, caesium, cui sane magna est in mento cicatrix' . . .   (*Ad Herennium* IV.xlix.63)

---

[33] [Cicero], *Ad C. Herennium Libri IV de Ratione Dicendi*, translated by H. Caplan (London, 1964), 1.2.3. *Elocutio* means style: 'the adaptation of suitable words and sentences to the matter devised.' The Ciceronian authorship of *Ad Herennium* had been challenged in the fifteenth century, by Lorenzo Valla and others, but in the sixteenth century it was still considered Ciceronian. It certainly was the basis of Stanihurst's rhetorical training.

[34] Giraldus Cambrensis, *Expugnatio Hibernica*, edited and translated by A. B. Scott and F. X. Martin (Dublin, 1978). Hereafter referred to as *Expugnatio*.

[Portrayal consists in representing and depicting in words clearly enough for recognition the bodily form of some person, as follows: 'I mean him, men of the jury, the ruddy, short, bent man, with white and rather curly hair, blue-grey eyes, and a huge scar on his chin' . . .]

Giraldus's picture of Raymond, however, is medieval and blunt, and not very flattering. Raymond Fitzgerald is something of a hero for Stanihurst: he was one of those who brought English rule to Ireland and Stanihurst was a tutor to one of his descendants. Our author therefore sets out to refine both the portrayal and the Latin.

'Quantitas' (*Expugnatio* 152) is a post-Augustan word, not used for a person's size, and in any case not refined enough for a good Ciceronian like Stanihurst. It is also unflattering (FitzGerald's nickname was Raymond le Gros). Stanihurst simply omits mention of Raymond's girth and makes him 'long and tall'. But in doing so I think he falsifies the account. This is what I meant above, when I said that his *imitatio* leads him astray.

Referring to Raymond's hair, Giraldus uses the word from *Ad Herennium*, 'subcrispus'. Stanihurst goes one better by making Raymond 'cincinnatus' (having curled hair), availing himself of a word attested in Cicero.[35]

'Oculis grossis et rotundis' is a phrase which is obviously Giraldus's own. It is a blunt description of Raymond's bulging eyes, and the language is certainly not drawn from any classical model. Stanihurst follows Giraldus, but uses the words 'eminens', which he gets from Cicero,[36] and 'caesius', which he gets from the *Ad Herennium*, although he cannot have been sure that Raymond had blue–grey eyes.

Raymond's 'rather prominent nose' (*Expugnatio*) becomes 'incurvatum', adapted from the 'incurvus' of the *Ad Herennium*; Stanihurst's description is again rather more flattering, but how does he know that Raymon's nose was 'bent slightly sideways'? Giraldus was a de Barri, and a cousin of Raymond FitzGerald: if he did not baulk at mentioning his bulk and his bulging eyes and big nose, he would surely have said if the nose was bent. I think that our author was looking at his model, noting that there was another element in the series ('scar on his chin'), and decided that he could add the element of physical disfigurement by bending the nose sideways. Once again, the training in *imitatio* is stronger than Stanihurst's desire to be true to his source.

The second passage I wish to discuss with reference to Stanihurst's lexis comes from the dedicatory letter at the beginning of *De Rebus*. Stanihurst complains that people on the continent have a bad impression of Ireland: this is because the nobility will not travel, and those who do travel are, for the most part, native Irish of the lower classes who beg their way to Rome in order to gain advancement in the Church. He says that this is so common

---

[35] Cicero, *Pro Sestio*, 11.26.
[36] Cicero, *In Vatinium 2*.

that the Romans, when they meet an Irish beggar, ask him 'My Lord, do you
intend to become a bishop?'[37] To illustrate this class he draws a brilliant
satiric pen-picture of 'Cornelius', an uneducated Irish priest embarking on
this quest:

> Hic igitur noster Cornelius, simul illius animus ambitionis aestu tumet, ex
> patrio nidulo comatus ac braccatus, sed vix commode calceatus in remotas
> nationes evolat.   (*De Rebus* 8)

> [Here then is our Cornelius: as soon as his spirit swells with the fervour
> of ambition he flies from his small paternal nest, heading for far off
> peoples, hairy and wearing breeches but scarcely well shod.]

'Comatus' and 'braccatus' are good Ciceronian words with resonances for
Stanihurst's classically educated audience. The first would suggest *Gallia
Comata*,[38] the urban (Roman) view of the shaggy (Celtic) barbarians north of
the Alps, and the second recalls the reference of Cicero to the 'trousered
Transalpine tribes',[39] or even the 'trousered throng of Goths' of whom Ovid
complained.[40] The classical references serve to intensify the satire on this
unkempt person, but what is notable is that they describe an Irish mode of
dress of the sixteenth and seventeenth centuries: the Irish did wear their hair
long and they dressed in tight-fitting trousers (known in English as trews),
which the well-hosed Elisabethan gentry found shockingly immodest.[41] In this
case, the Ciceronian *imitatio* serves Stanihurst very well: the classical language
serves to describe a contemporary scene.

It is noteworthy that Stanihurst's dislike of 'Cornelius' is based on class,
not on race. He despises what he perceives to be a lack of education and
urban sophistication, but he will have no part in the demonizing of the Irish,
a tradition which goes back at least to Giraldus Cambrensis and was particularly virulent in Stanihurst's time. This brings me to my second heading.

STANIHURST THE PALESMAN

After a general description of Ireland and its division into provinces,
Stanihurst comes to talk of another, political division of the country:

> Observare diligenter oportebit hiberniam in duas partes distributam esse,
> in Anglicam et Hibernicam: hanc germani, et genuini Hiberni, illam
> Anglorum progenies incolit; eaque portio, plebeio sermone, Anglica

---

[37] *De Rebus* 8: 'Domine, visne Episcopari?'
[38] Cicero, *Philippics* 8.9.27.
[39] Cicero, *Epistulae ad Familiares* 9.15.2.
[40] *Tristia* 4.6.47.
[41] See H. F. McClintock, *Old Irish and Highland Dress* (Dundalk, 1949), 49.

provincia nominatur, quod sit Anglorum territoriis, quasi palis et septis circumsessa.   (*De Rebus* 27)

[It will be fitting to observe carefully that Ireland is divided into two parts, the English and the Irish: the latter is inhabited by the true and genuine Irish, the former by the descendants of the English; and that portion, in the speech of the people is called the English province, because it is surrounded by the lands of the English as if by palings and fences.]

This is the beginning of another ethnography, a description of the Pale. The methodology is as outlined above (2–3). There is an account of its position, its extent, and its boundaries; of the success of its agriculture due to skill and toil, and a characterization of its inhabitants, their origin and migration, their difference from the native Irish, and their preservation of the pure English tongue: 'they preserve uncorrupted the antiquity of the English language'.[42]

Stanihurst's own example of the antiquity and purity of the English used in the Pale, his translation of the first four books of Virgil's *Aeneid*, was greeted with derision by his contemporaries because of its strange diction.[43] For example, these are the opening lines of book 4:

> But the Queene in meane while with carks quandare deepe anguisht
> Her wound fed by Venus, with firebayt smoldred is hooked.
> Thee wights doughtye manhood leagd with gentilytye nobil,
> His woords fitlye placed, with his heunly phisnomye pleasing,
> March through her hert mustring, al in her brest deepelye she
>   printeth.[44]

If the people of the Pale spoke an English even remotely resembling this, they surely were distinct both from the native Irish and the English. Stanihurst professes to know no Irish (Gaelic), but he is keen to point out that he admires the language and displays an understanding of the reluctance of the Irish to speak English:

Atqui, hoc loco, festivum illud Oreli responsum (est autem is, inter Hibernicos, clarus et nobilis) praeterire nolo. Hic, cum haberet infantem filium quattuor annos natum, qui balbus seu potius mutus erat, cumque alumni altrix parentem huius haesitantiae admoneret, dixisse fertur: A nobis igitur ad Anglicam provinciam amandetur, et ibi discat Anglice loqui.   (*De Rebus* 30)

---

[42] 'Incorruptam Anglicae linguae vetustatem servant', *De Rebus* 28.
[43] See W. B. Stanford, *Ireland and the Classical Tradition* (Dublin, 1984), 162–3.
[44] van der Haar, *Richard Stanyhurst's Aeneis*, 118.

[At this point I do not wish to pass over the witty response of a famous
Irish nobleman named O'Reilly. He had an infant son, four year old, who
stammered to the point of being dumb; when the wet nurse of the child
reported this impediment to the parent he is said to have replied 'let him
be sent from us into the English province, and there let him learn to
speak English'.]

I digress, but for two reasons. One is to note that digression, usually for the
purpose of introducing a witty anecdote, is a feature of Stanihurst's style;
consider the first words of the next passage quoted: *De Rebus* is dotted with
formulae like this, by which Stanihurst recalls himself to the main line of his
discourse. The other is to point out that although Stanihurst identifies with
the community of the Pale, he is by no means antagonistic to the native Irish.
However, his desire to mark the Palesmen as a distinct community, loyal to
the British crown, leads him to make an extreme statement. In language
almost that of apartheid he continues, coining the word 'Anglo-Irish':

> Sed ut inceptum opus persequamur, hi, quos iam in manibus habemus,
> Anglo-Hiberni, adeo sunt ab antiquis istis Hibernicis dissociati, ut colono-
> rum omnium ultimus, qui in Anglica provincia habitat, filiam suam vel
> nobilissimo Hibernicorum principi in matrimonium non daret. . . . Cives
> et municipales, more institutoque Anglorum, vivunt: auctoritate nutuque
> Britannicarum legum rempublicam administrant.   (*De Rebus* 30)

> [But to pursue the task we have begun, the people we are now dealing
> with, the Anglo-Irish, are so dissociated from those old Irish that the least
> of the tenant farmers who lives in the English province would not give
> his daughter in marriage even to the most noble chieftain among the
> Irish. . . . Citizens and burghers, they live by the custom and way of life of
> Englishmen: they govern the state by the authority and command of
> British laws.]

The very word 'Anglo-Irish' is indicative of a tension which pervades *De
Rebus*. The tension arises out of the circumstances of the Normans who
invaded Ireland: the more successful they were, the more they suffered from
the suspicion of the king of England that they might set up a separate kingdom. For example, in 1170, not long after the beginning of the conquest,
according to Giraldus Cambrensis, Maurice FitzGerald made a speech rally-
ing the Normans to go to the rescue of Robert FitzStephen. In the course of
this speech he uttered the words:

> Surely we do not look to our own people for succour? We are now con-
> strained in our actions by this circumstance, that just as we are English as
> far as the Irish are concerned, likewise to the English we are Irish, and the

inhabitants of this island and the other assail us with an equal degree of hatred.[45]

Stanihurst follows this, giving it a more classical turn:

> Et quidem vide, quantae curae illis nostra sit salus, cum, regis edicto, aqua et igni nobis interdicatur. Ea enim iam nostra ratio est, et is temporum cursus, ut sicut Hibernicis Angli, sic et Anglis Hibernici sumus. Horum odio, illorum armis premimur. (*De Rebus* 116)

> [And indeed, see how much our safety matters to them when, by the king's edict we are banished. Such is our situation now, and such the course of circumstance that just as we are English to the Irish, so are we Irish to the English. We are hard pressed by the hatred of the latter, by the arms of the former.]

The problems of maintaining a relationship with the mother country did not go away in the centuries after the conquest. This means that Stanihurst can read Giraldus with reference to the problems of his own community, and this indeed he does. Being a writer of considerable literary sophistication, he actually anticipates this criticism, that people will say he is interpreting history for his own purposes:

> Nec enim hanc orationem meam latius vagari, sed terminis illius tantum temporis circumscribi volo, quo Hiberni sub Britannorum imperium, et ditionem ceciderunt. Quandoquidem malos quosdam latinitatis interpretes non defuturos praevideo, qui singulis libelli mei syllabis, literarum tendiculis, insidiari, et omnia minima puncta peiorem ad partem verbi depravatione rapere pertentabunt. Quare Henrici consultationem oratione explico, ab eius posteritate mentem et manum cohibeo. (*De Rebus* 140–1)

> [Nor do I wish this discourse of mine to be too wide ranging. I want it to be confined solely within the bounds of that period, in which the Irish fell under the rule and writ of the British. For truly I foresee that certain wicked interpreters of Latin will not be lacking, who will lie in wait for every syllable of my modest book with their literary traps, and by distorting the word will put the worst interpretation on every tiny point. For this reason I outline Henry's deliberation in my discourse: I withhold my judgement and my pen from his descendants.]

This *apologia* is embedded in a long passage which describes King Henry's deliberations on appointing a vice-regent to Ireland. The following points are (rather tortuously) made:

---

[45] *Expugnatio* 81. Maurice was referring to the fact that Henry had issued and edict banning ships from taking supplies to Ireland, and ordering all his subjects to return.

1. Homini autem peregrino, nullo usu tractandae reipublicae imbuto, insulae adhuc vacillantis gubernacula tradere cum summo incommodo . . .
   coniunctum videbatur.   (*De Rebus* 138)

   [To hand over the governorship of an island, which was still wavering in
   its allegiance, to a foreigner endowed with no experience of dealing with
   that state seemed to involve the greatest disadvantage.]

   Ita necesse est . . . naufragia fieri, ubi homines inscientes, nulliusque
   ordinis venas tenentes, ad provinciae munia, temeraria electione,
   adhibentur.   (*De Rebus* 139)

   [Thus it is inevitable that . . . disasters will happen when unskilled men,
   who have no feel for any rank of society, are given administrative positions
   in the provinces through rash selection.]

2. Veterans who had won the province, men such as Strongbow, FitzStephen
   and FitzGerald, whose courage and loyalty were beyond question, would
   be offended and might cause trouble for the new governor, to make him
   lose favour with the king.

3. Cum externus homo provinciam accipit, accolas oportet eius benevolentiam
   honorariis colligere. Pluribus etiam accensis et sequestribus est succinctus,
   qui vocem habent venalem, quorum amicitiae fluxae sunt et suffragatoriae.
   Item coniunx, si constrictus sit uxore, muneribus est delinienda [*sic*].
   Siquidem blanda est stomachantis viri conciliatricula mulier, et plus
   interdum in pulvinari nocturna calantica quam in eo foro, in quo iuris
   nundinatio exercetur, vetusta membrana valet. (*De Rebus* 142)

   [When a man from outside takes over a province, the inhabitants have
   to procure his goodwill with gifts. Also he is surrounded by a crowd of
   attendants and agents, whose influence is for sale and whose friendships
   are fluid and relative. Likewise his wife, if he is shackled to a wife, has to
   be soothed with gifts. For a woman can sweetly coax an irritable man, and
   sometimes the fetching nightcap on his pillow has more effect than the
   musty paper in the court where the trafficking in the law is carried on.]

4. Omnes sane ad provincias confluunt eo solum consilio, ut magnos sibi
   quaestus instituant.   (*De Rebus* 142)

   [All of them, truly, flood into the provinces with one purpose only, to
   establish large profits for themselves.]

5. Iam vero, cum gubernatorum imperium non sit in insula statarium,
   imo saepius bimum, raro amplius trimum exsistat, aliique ut moris est,
   succedant: omnes fortunas quas in captanda benevolentia provinciales
   hactenus dissiparunt, iam nunc, mutatis rebus, coguntur amittere atque

novis muneribus designatos novosque magistratus et eius adstipulatores demulcere. Unde consequitur provinciales indigenas, ubi eorum bona, summo labore quaesita et collecta, exteri homines comesse solent, in horribiles miserias incurrere et ponderoso inopiae egestatisque pressu intoleranter gravescere. (*De Rebus* 142)

[Moreover since the command of governors on the island is not permanent but rather, more often consists of a two-, rarely more than a three-year term, and others succeed as is the custom, the provincials are forced to lose all the fortunes which they have squandered up to this point in gaining his good will and, now that things have changed, to woo with new gifts the new appointees to office, and their henchmen. The result is that the native provincials fall into wretched misery and are intolerably burdened by the weighty pressure of poverty and want, since their goods, toilsomely acquired and amassed, are continually consumed by outsiders.]

The whole account of King Henry's deliberation is an invention of Stanihurst. Giraldus conveys the fact, the result of Henry's thought, only in a chapter heading: 'Earl Richard [i.e. Strongbow] sent to Ireland as governor'.[46] It is worthwhile, therefore, to pay attention to what arguments Stanihurst chooses to use.

Points (1) and (2) are anchored in the period of the conquest by the mention of names (Henry, Strongbow, FitzStephen, etc.), but even within (1) the switch in tenses in the passages quoted is significant: 'seemed to involve' is historic and might well have been in Henry's mind, but 'it is inevitable' is present tense and generalizing, and therefore applicable to Stanihurst's own time. It is, I think, an indication of the resentment that people like Stanihurst's own father must have felt when they saw their own Parliament being superseded, and governors appointed from London.[47]

The whole deliberation is supposed to have taken place in 1173, some six years after the Norman invasion of Ireland. But Henry had never previously appointed a vice-regent and therefore cannot have witnessed the behaviour described in points (3), (4), and (5). This, along with the constant generalizing use of the present tense, indicates that what we have here is an account of the behaviour of corrupt and greedy officials visited upon Ireland after the recall of Sir Henry Sidney in 1571.[48] Earlier in *De Rebus* Stanihurst records a eulogy, in elegiac couplets, of Sidney which he, Stanihurst, had written about the time when Sidney had added to the buildings in Dublin Castle, i.e. about 1570.

---

[46] *Expugnatio* 135.
[47] Cf. supra, p1.
[48] 'There was . . . an assumption . . . that Ireland was a colony with opportunities for gain and advancement for those who were willing to adventure for them.' C. Brady and R. Gillespie (eds), *Natives and Newcomers: Essays on the Making of Irish Colonial Society, 1534–1641* (Dublin, 1986), 16–17.

Verum Sidnaei laudes haec saxa loquuntur . . .   (*De Rebus* 22)

[Truly these stones speak the praises of Sidney.]

The combination of this nostalgic praise for Sidney and the contempt displayed for later governors is, I think, significant of what Stanihurst desires:
an Ireland governed by the aristocracy of the Pale, maintaining a dignified
rapport with the British crown.

Another passage in which Stanihurt expands on his source gives us an
insight into his feelings at the way he himself was treated. Giraldus recounts,
rather casually, how Hervey de Montmorency brought a false charge of
treason against Raymond Fitzgerald: 'Hervey . . . whose new connection with
the [FitzGerald] family had not altered his customary malice, sent messages
to the king of England that events had taken an ominous turn.'[49]

The treatment of this episode in *De Rebus* is much more elaborate. Stanihurst purports to give the contents of Hervey's letter, outlining the insinua-
tions by which Hervey tried to win the king's grace for himself and to
incriminate Raymond. The insight is, of course, Stanihurst's own invention.

He then goes on to say that King Henry was too ready to lend credence to
the accusations, and adds a rhetorical question:

An quod, in laesae maiestatis delatione, omnis accusatorum oratio aditum
ad principum aures facillime habeat?   (*De Rebus* 162).

[Was this because, in a delation of treason, every speech of the accusers
most easily finds access to the ears of princes?]

I have deliberately left the word 'delation' in my translation to draw attention
to Stanihurst's choice of vocabulary: not 'accusatio', not 'crimen' or 'incrim-
inatio', but 'delatio' with, at least for Stanihurst's audience, its sinister
Tacitean overtones and its implication of informers and the reign of terror.[50]
Note also the switch into the present tense: our author is not confining his
analysis to the period of the Norman Conquest, but is making a universal
statement applicable to his own time and circumstances.

There follows a long *excursus in calumniatores bene meritorum civium* (*De
Rebus* 162, marginale), a digression on those who bring false charges against
respectable citizens. This is a carefully worked and highly rhetorical passage.
In the first part Stanihurst, as it were, summons before him the person of
the 'calumniator' in a series of indignant questions: if we look only at the
first one we can learn something more about his training in rhetoric.[51]

---

[49] *Expugnatio* 159.
[50] Cf. Tacitus, *The Histories*, trans. D. S. Levene (Oxford, 1997), 4, 'Nor were the informers more hated for
their crimes than for their prizes; . . . some . . . won administrative office and a place at the heart of power.'
[51] See note 31.

Nam cum homines, intra leges viventes, legis praesidio armari debeant, tu quis es, qui bono bonorum praemia adimere, aut civi minime malo malorum supplicia proponere audeas?   (*De Rebus* 162)

[. . . while men living within the law ought to be protected by the bulwark of the law, *who are you*[52] who dare to deprive the good citizen of the rewards of the good, or to propse the punishments of the wicked for a citizen who is by no means a criminal.]

Within the sentence, note the use of metaphor (*praesidio armari*) and the carefully worked antithesis[53] (*bono–malo; bonorum–malorum; praemia–supplicia*). Stanihurst is exerting himself in the matter of style. The figure of antithesis is set in a series of questions addressed to an unnamed person, the figure called 'apostrophe' in the *Ad Herennium*.[54] The series of questions which follows is another figure of thought, called *ratiocinatio*.[55] (From the footnotes it will be seen how closely together these are treated in the *Ad Herennium*: it is easy to see where Stanihurst went for guidance in matters of style.)

The burden of the questions is the plight of the helpless citizen caught in the toils of false charges brought by some powerful man who is motivated solely by malice.

. . . civem, a legibus digitu nusquam discedentem, lege, sine lege, tamquam maleficum mirmillonem iugulare.   (*De Rebus* 163)

[Lawlessly to use the law to hang a citizen, who never stirred a finger's breadth outside the law, as if he were an evildoer condemned for violent crime.]

The second part of the digression is a plea that attacks on the innocent be banned. It develops into a eulogy on the principle of innocence and ends with an impassioned declaration:

Magno igitur opere, omnes qui ad gubernacula reipublicae sedent providere debent, ne praeposteri et immanitate efferati emissarii in viros, innocentia tectos et legibus septos, odium iniquissime struant et in primis ne iuris operimento domesticas inimicitias tegere et velare audeant.   (*De Rebus* 164)

---

[52] My italics.

[53] *Ad Herennium* 4.15.21, 'Embellishing our style by means of this figure we shall be able to give it impressiveness and distinction.'

[54] *Ad Herennium* 4.15.22, 'Apostrophe is the figure which expresses grief or indignation by means of an address to some man . . .'; this is also treated at 4.53.66 under the name Personification (*conformatio*): 'Personification consists in representing an absent person as present.'

[55] *Ad Herennium* 4.16.23. Reasoning be question and answer. This follows immediately upon another figure called interrogation.

[Therefore, all who sit at the helm of the commonwealth ought to take great care that perverse informers, rendered bestial by their savagery, should not bring odium on men protected by their innocence and fenced about by the law; and especially that they should not dare to cover and conceal their private enmities with a cloak of right.]

Stanihurst then, rather endearingly, brings himself back to his narrative with the words 'If Henry had turned over such thoughts in his mind, he would easily have quashed the complaints of Hervey'. But it seems clear that our author must be referring to the turbulent politics of the Counter-Reformation and the 'Irish Question', and indeed he had himself had personal experience of false charges. In 1573, one Robert Lalor, a steward of the FitzGeralds, earls of Kildare, laid information in Dublin that Stanihurst was involved in a plot to transport the young earl to Spain with a view to marrying him to a daughter of Philip II and bringing him back to be Philip's viceroy in Ireland. There was no truth in the matter, but it came back to haunt Stanihurst in 1580 when he was in London. He came under suspicion because of his association with Edmund Campion and was questioned by the earl of Leicester. Leicester also had his earlier record searched and received a report from Archbishop Loftus and Chancellor Gerrard in Dublin that Stanihurst was 'an ill member of the common weal'.[56]

Once again, we observe the method: although there is no overt criticism of the English administration of his own day, Stanihurst takes an incident from the *Expugnatio* and uses it as a starting point for a generalizing comment on the difficulties of the community of the Pale in its alienation from the crown.

The Stanihurst who emerges from the pages of *De Rebus* is a complex man, a scholar, philosopher, alchemist, historian, and notable Latin stylist. Although he was an exile in the Spanish Netherlands when he was writing, he preserved a vision of an Ireland unified in a common culture by education, not conquest and colonization, and governed by the aristocracy of the Pale, a community marked by the qualities that he found in the Normans of the *Expugnatio*: courage, knowledge of the ways of the native Irish, skill in administration, and loyalty to the British crown.

Even as he wrote, Stanihurst must have been aware that his dream was impossible. However, the insights that he brings from his reading of Giraldus Cambrensis, insights into the problems of a community trying to maintain a dignified relationship with the metropolis, are still of interest today because the Irish Question has still not been answered. Giraldus could speak to Stanihurst: Stanihurst can speak to us.

University College, Cork

---

[56] Lennon, *Richard Stanihurst*, 36–7.

2

John Owen the epigrammatist: a literary and historical context

BYRON HARRIES

To be born in the third quarter of the sixteenth century into a family proud of both its Welsh cultural heritage and its Catholic recusancy, at the moment when even schoolmasters were again being required by law to assent to the Act of Supremacy, was a challenging start.[1] The family, landowners in the principality and active in its local politics, had supplied young men to train abroad for the Catholic priesthood, and almost certainly offered hiding-places for recusant clergy active in their area, with one family member already indicted and under penalty for the old religion. Like his brother, our subject is first tutored at home, eventually going up to Oxford in the early 1580s and turning to a career in the law. Advancement requires patronage, so he detaches himself in a public way from his known Catholic affiliations, becomes an apologist for the Established Church, and writes propaganda on its behalf, while at the same time resisting at this stage the call to enlist among its clergy. He is tempted elsewhere; as an enthusiastic advocate of Roman poetry, especially the social satirists Horace, Juvenal, and Martial, he begins to write so-called 'imitations', contemporary in their subject matter but obviously influenced by continental Roman poetics. By 1610 his Anglican public identity is established, along with his new 'Britishness', which is formed, in the best Tudor tradition, out of a radical re-writing of the old;[2] patrons support him in respectable offices in return for the dedication of successive books of verse; these books secure their author's reputation in his lifetime, and he can even offer flattering poems to a potential sovereign, the

[1] The sources from which this opening paragraph is constructed are: R. C. Bald, *John Donne, A Life* (Oxford, 1970); E. Gwynne Jones, 'The Lleyn recusancy case, 1578–1581', *The Transactions of the Honourable Society of Cymmrodorion*, session 1936 (London, 1937), 97–123; J. Henry Jones, 'John Owen, *Cambro-Britannus*', *The Transactions of the Honourable Society of Cymmrodorion*, session 1940 (London, 1941), 130–43; J. Henry Jones, 'John Owen, the epigrammatist', *Greece and Rome*, 10 (1941), 65–73; T. D. Kendrick, *British Antiquity* (London, 1950); David Mathew, *The Celtic Peoples and Renaissance Europe* (London, 1933); D. Aneurin Thomas, *The Welsh Elizabethan Catholic Martyrs* (Cardiff, 1971); I quote Owen's poems from the London collected edition of 1633, referring to them by their number within each of the ten books, which are identified as follows: (1606) 1–3; the Neville collection; (1607); the Arabella Stuart *liber singularis*; (1612) 1–3; the books dedicated to Henry, prince of Wales (1–2) and Charles, duke of York (3); (1613) 1–3; the Noel, Sidley, and Roger Owen collections.
[2] Kendrick, *British Antiquity*, 34–44.

short-lived Henry, prince of Wales. His fame confirmed by an engraved portrait, he dies in his fifties and is buried in the old St Paul's, where grateful patrons erect an effigy. In the following decades, his poems continue to be printed and carry his reputation well into the next century.

John Owen liked playing tricks on his audience, disorienting them not with the merely unexpected but in the ludic manner, with the very opposite of what their inductive sense leads them to expect, and so subverting the predictable course of the rational thought-process on which he simultaneously depends. He may therefore have appreciated this introduction, recognizing in the mirror of the narrative's carefully contrived selectivity a double image, not only his own but also that of his contemporary John Donne, whom the details also fit more or less exactly, and in whose poetry – along with that of others whom Samuel Johnson would term 'Metaphysicals' – it will be my contention that we find the point of reference most helpful for coming to terms with Owen's achievement today. As in the best ludic recognition-tricks (Owen knew this too), differences between the two poets serve only to enhance the points of similarity, and so I shall first acknowledge the more obvious biographical discrepancies.

Donne was not actually born in Wales, and his strong Welsh connections are only on his father's side,[3] just as the Catholicism in the family was primarily due to the influence of his mother, a direct descendant of Sir Thomas More's sister.[4] Donne took longer to shake off his Catholic inheritance than Owen,[5] which explains why Owen was not only able to matriculate but took a degree after the required four years of residence and subscribed to the Established Church. Donne left after three years without a degree,[6] travelled abroad as an adventurer, married (notoriously, with deep personal commitment), and eventually succumbed in 1615 with great reluctance to patronal pressure to take orders in the Church.

---

[3] Possibly in Carmarthenshire (Bald, *John Donne*, 20–2), though connections may have existed with the Herberts of Montgomeryshire (23). Except for reporting the claims of Donne himself or of Wotton Walton's *Life* is scarcely reliable; for a literary context in which to evaluate his achievement, see now J. Martin, *Walton's Lives: Conformist Commemorations and the Rise of Biography* (Oxford, 2002). Donne's birth can be dated to 1572 (Bald, *John Donne*, 35).

[4] Bald, *John Donne*, 22–6. The father's early death ensured the priority of Catholic influence in the son's education, 36–8; for the family priests and Jesuit connections 23–6. Donne's maternal uncle, Jasper Heywood, was a Jesuit missionary priest indicted for high treason in February 1584 (41–2) and imprisoned in the Tower (44–5), who 'unquestionably . . . got in touch with members of his family in England' and 'may even have taken refuge from time to time under his sister's roof. The children must have seen and spoke to him, and no doubt he made a deep impression on them' (39–40).

[5] By his own testimony in *Pseudo-Martyr* ('I had a longer work to doe than many other men . . .'), Bald, *John Donne*, 39; early education at home 38, with brother, Henry 42.

[6] The Donne brothers had matriculated at Hart Hall (i.e. Hertford College) in 1584, but being under sixteen were not required to take the Oath of Supremacy (Bald, *John Donne*, 42); John left after three years, perhaps to avoid the Oath on reaching that age (46), four years being necessary for the B.A. (45, note 3). When Owen matriculated at New College at about the same time as the Donnes, he was already of the age when submission to the Oath was required by statute, having spent five years at Winchester since his domestic tutoring had ended at the age of thirteen; see J. H. Jones, '*Cambro-Britannus*', 133–4.

Owen did none of these; as far as we know, he never left these shores, never married, and consistently refused ordination, despite the obvious career advantages for a successful school headmaster and the opportunities for preferment it conferred. Above all, even Donne's Martial imitations and other epigrams and satires were from the first in English, while Owen's published verse was all in Latin. The language made a vital difference: while Donne's death (1631) was followed by the publication of his collected poems in London, editions which gave him a national reputation,[7] Owen's death in 1622[8] saw his posthumous reputation grow from a national one (four published books of verses in his lifetime) to one extended throughout Protestant Europe by the Dutch printing presses; he would be reprinted by rationalists in the German Enlightenment and in Paris during the Revolution, at the height of the anti-clerical terror.[9]

Donne and Owen were virtual contemporaries at Oxford, where it has been not implausibly suggested that they met through the agency of Owen's fellow Wykehamist, Henry Wotton, a lifelong friend of Donne's.[10] If so, Owen's distancing himself from his domestic Catholic origins in these years may have made him wary of too intimate a friendship with his precocious fellow student. Much the same pattern persists in London, where Owen spent at least the last fourteen years of his life with patrons of poetry in literary circles, mostly before Donne finally took orders, though Donne would have been based in parishes outside London for the last six of those years. At a distance from each other, they are known to have shared many important and influential friends.[11] These parallels in the two lives are more than merely fortuitous. In both, the need to assert an independence from family and 'dubious' background fuelling suspicions of treason was a driving force in the early years, and may well have contributed to the strong reluctance in both to take advantage of the obvious benefits conferred by ordination in the Anglican Church, though both energetically campaigned with propaganda on its behalf; and if both made tentative first steps in the legal profession, only to beat a quick retreat, was this because both might easily, given the frenetic atmosphere of the 1590s, have found themselves engaged in legal suppression of their former co-religionists?

I shall return to Donne presently, but first I must stress the hot-house atmosphere of intrigue, religious intransigence, conspiracy, and even covert treason which the young Owen left behind at home when he went (briefly)

---

[7] Bald, *John Donne*, 550.

[8] The date given by Wood in *Athenae Oxonienses* (1691), I, 400; J. H. Jones, however ('*Cambro-Britannus*', 135), is doubtful, speculating that Owen may have lived to 1627–8, but without sufficient reason. The evidence from St Paul's was destroyed in the Great Fire.

[9] 1794, in a splendid two-volume edition.

[10] Bald, *John Donne*, 43, using Walton.

[11] The case of Sir Henry Goodyear is highlighted by Bald, *John Donne*, 153–4 and J. H. Jones, '*Cambro-Britannus*', 136–7. I shall list others in my concluding paragraphs.

to Winchester before going up to New College, a progress he proudly celebrates in a later poem.[12] His family, the Owens of Plas Du on the Llŷn peninsula, were among the lesser gentry of the county, and like others of their
kind at Madryn, Cefnamwlch, and Pennarth, actively promoted the Catholic
religion,[13] believing (as State Papers record) that 'their own solidarity and
their remoteness from Bangor [the see] would secure them against the
inquisitiveness of diocesan visitors'.[14] The founding in the 1570s of colleges
at Douai, Rheims, and Rome to train British students for the Catholic priesthood, and send them back to serve and encourage the small communities of
faithful laity, proved to be an incentive for young men from these gentry
families in North Wales to seek their education abroad with this potentially
treasonable career in mind. During Elizabeth's reign, over fifty young men
from the remoter regions of North Wales and Chester went as students to
the colleges on the Continent, and thirty-three returned to work on 'the
Mission'.[15] Gentry houses like Plas Du provided sanctuary and hospitality.
Thomas Owen, John's father, maintained a staunchly Catholic household,[16]
and two of John's uncles, Hugh and Robert, went to test their vocations
overseas.[17]

   The world of secret liturgies and pious practices, with talk of 'Yr hen ffydd'
(the old religion), saints' lives, mariolatry, and pilgrimages to holy wells,
shrines, and monastic sites on the peninsula, would have been part of young
John's experience. Why, then, did he not join his uncles abroad? There must
have been a moment of decisive rejection, though, as in Donne's case, this
was doubtless part of a longer process of acclimatization to the new religion.
His going up to Oxford proves nothing in itself, as the university provided
a stepping-stone for scores of young men who followed the distinguished
fellow of St John's, Edmund Campion, abroad and into the Catholic priesthood. A Welsh student there could look to the examples of Owen Lewis of

[12] (1612) 3.64.

[13] Full background with bibliography in Thomas, *Welsh Catholic Martyrs*, 9–46; fullest details of these families
in E. G. Jones, 'The Lleyn recusancy', 97–103. John Owen's aunt, Agnes Owen, married Thomas Madryn (100,
pedigree 123), whose family had connections with Morris Clynnog, rector of the English College, Rome in
1578–9 (97 note 2).

[14] Thomas, *Welsh Catholic Martyrs*, 34.

[15] Thomas, *Welsh Catholic Martyrs*, 32, with a breakdown of the figures.

[16] It was to be alleged against him in 1578 that he had given refuge to six priests at Plas Du (E. G. Jones,
'The Lleyn recusancy', 103), and that sixteen members of his family could be 'accused of papistry' (122,
interrogatory 40).

[17] Hugh Owen almost certainly enjoyed a colourful early career in the service of the twelfth earl of Arundel
(Mathew, *The Celtic Peoples*, 232–7; 'not yet clearly proved', 233), backed the Armada (J. H. Jones, '*Cambro-
Britannus*', 131 with references) and was alleged to be complicit in the Gunpowder Plot (E. G. Jones, 'The
Lleyn recusancy', 101). A. H. Dodd (*Studies in Stuart Wales* [Cardiff, 1971], 45) claims he 'had a hand in every
plot against the heretic state'. According to an epitaph in the English College, Rome, he died on 28 May 1618
(J. H. Jones, '*Cambro-Britannus*', 131), and in his will made no provision for his apostate poet-nephew (135).
Robert Owen also enjoyed the patronage of the Arundel family (E. G. Jones, 'The Lleyn recusancy', 101), was
at Douai in 1570 and served as a priest on the continent, making occasional visits home to Wales (102–3).
Both brothers kept up a regular correspondence with Thomas Owen at Plas Du (102).

Anglesey, who had left Oxford to become a professor at Douai a decade earlier,[18] or to the principal of St Mary's Hall and fellow of Oriel, Morgan Phillips,[19] or to Robert Gwyn, also from Llŷn, who had graduated at Corpus in 1568 before going to Douai under Robert Owen's influence. Gwyn was ordained in 1575 and returned to work in North Wales, publishing Catholic apologetic material in Welsh and no doubt regularly visiting Plas Du.[20] Given this family background and network of Welsh Catholic sympathizers, why did John Owen not follow family members and friends overseas? I suggest a reason: very soon after his arrival as a teenage student at Winchester, his home at Plas Du was thrown into confusion by an event which I think terrified him.

For two decades, Catholic life among these remote gentry families had continued without serious interruption, though their identity and sympathies were known to the diocesan authorities.[21] State records show that in 1578–9, within months of young John Owen's admission to Winchester,[22] the Privy Council expressed increasing alarm at the 'state of religion' in Wales, drawing attention to how 'certain evil disposed persons, being sent from Rome and termed reconcilers, have crept among her highness' subjects of those parts and seduced many of them from the true religion established in this realm'.[23] The lord president of the Council of the Marches, Sir Henry Sidney, was told to conduct a full enquiry; the bishop of Bangor was ordered to raid the houses of Catholic sympathizers, among them the Owens' home at Plas Du. Thomas Owen, John's father, was arrested and indicted on serious charges of harbouring 'papistical persons' who had entered the country illegally from the Continent.[24] His family was among those, some of whom were already in prison at Ludlow, identified as 'knowne papists, and, as we hear, cheefe maintainers of that secte'.[25] Arrested on 29 July, Thomas was sent to Ludlow for trial and sentenced to imprisonment by the Council of the Marches. Application was granted for a retrial, but although he was indicted again in June 1579 by his local enemy, Richard Vaughan of Llwyndyrus, Carnguwch, whose rigorous pursuit of the Owens had contributed to his appointment as high sheriff in November of the previous year, proceedings appear to have lapsed, perhaps through the influence of other local families.[26]

[18] Mathew, *The Celtic Peoples*, 78–87.
[19] Thomas, *Welsh Catholic Martyrs*, 30.
[20] Thomas, *Welsh Catholic Martyrs*, 39–41.
[21] E. G. Jones, 'The Lleyn recusancy', 100–3; Thomas Owen had served as county sheriff in 1569.
[22] Recorded for 1577, at the age of thirteen (J. H. Jones, '*Cambro-Britannus*', 133 with references.
[23] Thomas, *Welsh Catholic Martyrs*, 33; frustration had been intensifying for a year or more, 22–3.
[24] Thomas, *Welsh Catholic Martyrs*, 33–4.
[25] E. G. Jones, 'The Lleyn recusancy', 98–9, with references to P.R.O., *State Papers, Domestic, Elizabeth*, 123/1 (cf. 123/11).
[26] E. G. Jones, 'The Lleyn recusancy', 104–7, with documentation 109–23 (P.R.O. *Star Chamber Proceedings, Elizabeth*, bundle 09, no. 18).

This action was an immediate success. Gentry families in the Llŷn peninsula not only became more lukewarm towards the nascent Catholic revival
they were helping to promote in the area, but some, like the Griffiths family
of Cefnamwlch, began to see advantages in conforming to the state church
and would, within a decade, be serving as county sheriffs.[27] There is no
record of such a change of heart at Plas Du, where the Owen family survived
by keeping a very low profile indeed, but the shock of what had happened
and the danger of those tempted to follow Robert Gwyn must have made a
deep impression on the young John Owen, sent to safety at Winchester, and
the path now being explored by the Griffiths and other neighbouring families will have seemed increasingly attractive to a vulnerable student not too
enamoured of martyrdom. Donne, by contrast, came from a family already
hardened against such pressures; a proud lineage of recusant fugitives and
martyrs will have stiffened his resolve not to conform merely out of fear
and expediency.[28]

That Owen's family sent him to Winchester in 1577 would not be entirely
due to these growing domestic tensions; he must have been thought suitable
for formal academic training, as he would be a pupil there under the formid-
able divine, Thomas Bilson. Other recusant families used the College for
their sons, as Bilson, despite his personal conformity (he was later to be
bishop of Winchester), seems to have taken a liberal outlook towards the
religion of his charges. At Oxford in the 1580s recusancy was notoriously an
issue of covert debate and personal mental anguish for many. Donne survived there as still a Catholic for three years, apparently without compromise,
and Owen's submission to the oath required on matriculation[29] should not
be taken to suggest an already transformed spiritual allegiance. Crucial steps
came with graduation and election to a college fellowship, to which Owen
proceeded in 1584, taking his BCL in 1590.[30] For a career he rejected law,
showed unusual reluctance to take orders, perhaps to avoid open conflict
with his family, and ended up as a schoolmaster, possibly inspired by Bilson's
example.[31] When he took up his first post, at Trelech in Monmouthshire, he
would have had to subscribe publicly to the Elizabethan Act of Supremacy.[32]
Certainly, the headship of the Henry VIII School at Warwick, which Owen
held for about a decade from the mid-1590s, was a prestigious Midlands

---

[27] Thomas Madryn, Thomas Owen's brother-in-law, was already sheriff in 1586 (Thomas, *Welsh Catholic Martyrs*, 35; E. G. Jones, 'The Lleyn recusancy', 107).

[28] For the rationale of Donne's submission to the established church, see Helen Gardner, 'The interpretation of Donne's sonnet on the church', *The Divine Poems of John Donne* (Oxford, 1978), 121, app. C. I owe this
reference to Christopher Armstrong.

[29] See note 6.

[30] J. H. Jones, '*Cambro-Britannus*', 134, 'The epigrammatist', 66. Owen's first published collection (1606)
identifies him as 'Collegii B. Mariae (quod vulgo *Novum* vocant) nuper Socius'.

[31] The debt was openly acknowledged in epigrams; (1606) 2.25 *Tu mihi praeceptor quondam, Bilsone, fuisti; /
Debeo praeceptis, scribo quod ista, tuis*, 2.27, (1612) 3.64.

[32] Under a provision of 1563, Thomas, *Welsh Catholic Martyrs*, 10.

position, open only to those who enjoyed powerful patronage, especially as Owen had no local connections there and no personal experience of the court in London.[33]

How did he solicit personal favour? Clearly by his published poetry, as his family connections would hardly have served him well, and the same circumstances which applied to Donne affected Owen. Many of even the most distinguished poets among the 'metaphysicals' could and did write in both Latin and English (Ben Jonson, Vaughan, Marvell), as did the religious lyricists (Herbert, Crashaw),[34] but it was unusual for a British poet of national reputation and enduring merit (unlike the academic versifiers who would feature in *Musae Anglicanae*[35]) to publish exclusively in Latin. Is Owen's preference to be explained by the simple fact that his first and native language was Welsh?[36] This is hardly likely. More than a dozen years at Winchester and Oxford would have instilled confidence in using English, in default of which the Warwick appointment is unthinkable.[37] Yet, it remains true that Welsh and Latin, the latter first accessible to him through the family's hearing Mass read regularly and their receiving the sacraments in the Roman rite, were the two languages which linked Owen to his home. If he rejected so much – family loyalty, the narrow perspective of a local culture, and a fiercely exclusive and protective religious allegiance – Latin will have remained the one link connecting his memories of distant Caernarvonshire not only with his later studies but with a whole academic discourse in contemporary English science and historiography,[38] as well as a European dimension which bound together all with access to Latin in a shared literary culture inherited from the Italian Renaissance.

That writers saw for themselves the opportunity of disseminating ideas abroad through Latin is evident from the choice of that language for the first edition of William Camden's great *Britannia*, surely a case for primary publication in the vernacular if ever there was one,[39] but they were also encouraged by patrons to seek this wider audience as part of the propagandizing

---

[33] J. H. Jones, '*Cambro-Britannus*', 134, 'The epigrammatist', 66.

[34] In general, L. Bradner, *Musae Anglicanae: A History of Anglo-Latin Poetry, 1500–1925* (New York, 1940), with studies in J. W. Binns (ed.), *The Latin Poetry of English Poets* (London, 1974); for a critical survey of seventeenth century poets, see D. K. Money, *The English Horace: Anthony Alsop and the Tradition of British Latin Verse* (Oxford, 1998), 7–53.

[35] For this and similar anthologies, see Money, *The English Horace*, 39–40.

[36] J. H. Jones's discussions ('*Cambro-Britannus*', 138–42, 'The epigrammatist', 72) suggest he may have thought this.

[37] Nor is it likely, as J. H. Jones, 'The epigrammatist', 68 proposed, that a distinctively Welsh influence plays a significant role in Owen's poetic *materia*. 'Accusations of bribery and injustice' are as common in medieval English and Anglo-Latin verse as in Tudor Welsh, and casuistical theologians are the regular targets of many sixteenth and seventeenth century continental (Protestant) Latin satirists.

[38] Much relevant material is impressively assembled in J. W. Binns, *Intellectual Culture in Elizabethan and Jacobean England: The Latin Writings of the Age* (Leeds, 1990).

[39] Though it must be remembered that the area covered by *Britannia* was, as Camden was well aware, still one of considerable linguistic diversity with no single tongue yet the predominant speech in every part.

projection of the image of a new, national British state throughout Europe. Clearly such an image, although given new impetus by the Union of the Kingdoms at the accession of James VI/I, had already been formed in the previous century, with the national, Anglican Church as an integral feature. It was promoted by ambassadors and merchants, and by major, long-nurtured scholarly achievements like Henry Savile's prestigious edition of John Chrysostom[40] as much as by military adventures against Spain in the Netherlands, and by encouraging Dutch and French Protestants to settle in England. Owen's trilingual background will have emphasized the symbolic significance, evident in university and literary circles, which Latin alone possessed as a truly national British language, as such immediately relevant to the promotion of the new national identity among the educated at home as well as overseas. No doubt he could have deployed his tricks of witty alliteration, name-play, and anagram in Welsh or, like many of his contemporaries (Shakespeare, Donne, and Jonson pre-eminent among them), in English.

The choice of Latin from the first alone matched the medium with the message, the national language with the national cause. Beyond this, Latin uniquely offered Owen access to the wider European reading public who would continue to appreciate him long after he was virtually forgotten at home. Nor was the advantage merely one of a convenient medium; Owen could wittily allude to the source of the themes he often derived from the prose satires of Erasmus, especially the pecuniary avarice of doctors and (Roman) prelates, the scholastic pedantry of old-fashioned lawyers and theologians, pretentiousness and ambition in self-seeking courtiers and socialites,[41] all stock-in-trade themes which Erasmian satire also transmitted to Rabelais and Molière, though not radically different from the familiar objects of Latin and vernacular satire in the fourteenth and fifteenth centuries.[42] Like many Protestant authors who helped to shape European Protestant culture in the seventeenth century, Owen skilfully exploited the anti-clerical tendencies which lay just under the surface of Erasmian satire, and his invoking of Lipsius, Casaubon, and Scaliger advertised his ambition to be considered a powerful influence on that culture.[43]

Owen's published corpus appeared between 1606 and 1613, three publications each of *Epigrammatum Libri Tres* in 1606, 1612, and 1613, with a *Liber Singularis* in 1607.[44] The concentrated publication of the collections at the

---

[40] Eton, 1612–13, in eight folio volumes, and still the standard critical edition of the largest collection of a single author's writings to survive from antiquity. Manuscript readings had been sought and supplied from many libraries in continental Europe. Owen celebrates its publication in (1612) 2.33.

[41] Erasmus's *Moriae Encomium* was widely known in England, not least through the popular translation by Thomas Chaloner (1549), with its satirical treatment of pedantic learning (49), lawyers (51), theologians (53), courtiers (56), and prelates (57–60). For Owen's ludic response to the work see (1606) 2.85 and (1612) 2.92.

[42] For the transmission, see A. J. Krailsheimer, *Rabelais and the Franciscans* (Oxford, 1963).

[43] On Erasmus (1612) 3.34, Scaliger (1606) 1.16, Lipsius (1612) 1.47.

[44] Appended to the 1607 set was an untypical assemblage of versified moral *dicta* derived from classical sources, *Monostica quaedam ethica et politica veterum sapientum*. As if to emphasize the difference in tone and the

beginning and end of this seven-year period suggests the gathering together of poems written over a considerable time and offered cumulatively in two pairs of publications. From the first, variety within each book was sought by the skilful ordering of successive poems. As there is no metrical variety, and only comparatively insignificant shift in tone and style, any critical comparison with Martial, who uses these and other techniques to achieve diversity, is really beside the point. Where Martial does confine himself to the elegiac couplet (as in the early *De Spectaculis*), his epigrams centre on a single set of circumstances which gives unity to the book while approaching the subject from different angles.[45] In Owen, by contrast, thematic variety of an often unexpected kind keeps the reader alert, along with verbal tricks, puns, even rhymes and name-play of a type which have much more in common with contemporary English 'metaphysicals' than with Roman poetics. Martial does use name-play, but his contrived etymologies are less superficial than Owen's, which can pun crudely, as when he writes of the island of Anglesey (*Mona*) near his home: 'Insula quam Taciti non tacuere libri'.[46]

The poem from which this comes ([1606] 3.39) is unusual in its length of eight couplets, in part explained by its royal addressee and position at the climax of a short sequence on a major theme, but also because it is followed by a footnote identifying several allusions and quoting a Welsh proverb.[47] This is no accidental surfacing of some hidden linguistic memory. Owen's references to the Welsh derivation of the island's name from Latin and to his own name in its vernacular form occur in the two central couplets, ensuring that the poet and his remote place of origin are privileged by position within an elaborate poetic celebration of the new nation state, and so determining the broader context within which the narrow references must now be read.

The obvious models for such a strategy are the poems in which Propertius, Horace, and Virgil record the names of their birthplaces by similarly recondite contrivances to give them added lustre within the wider Italian and imperial poetic themes.[48] As with his classical predecessors, Owen is finding

derivative nature of these 129 pieces, the collected editions detach them from the *Liber Singularis* and print them at the end. What is their origin? I suggest they may point to the way Owen trained himself in his art by turning into couplets moral observations he gathered from reading Cicero, Seneca, and others. The familiar model of the *Disticha Catonis* lay to hand in hexameters.

[45] In any case, only about one-quarter of the poems in *De spectaculis* are conventionally printed as distichs in modern editions, though none exceeds the six couplets which Owen normally allows himself as a maximum (making the eight of [1606] 3.39 all the more conspicuous and significant, as I explain below). Martial's very different techniques and presentational skills are extensively explored in J. P. Sullivan, *Martial, the Unexpected Classic* (Cambridge, 1991).

[46] The allusion, of course, is to Tacitus' account (*Ann.* 14.29–30) of the assault on the Druidic settlement on Anglesey by Suetonius Paulinus in AD 60.

[47] '*Proverbium Brittan. Mon mam Gymri*' (sc. 'Anglesey, mother of Wales'). This secures a mention for Wales and her poet in laying out the major theme, the historical appropriateness of the *tergeminum Britanniae imperium* achieved by the union of the crowns in 1603, as the note explains.

[48] Propertius 1.22, Horace *Odes* 3.30, and Virgil *Georgics* 3.10–15 are cases Owen would know well. The Virgilian self-reference is also placed at the centre of the whole poem.

a new place and significant role for local identity within the emerging concept of national *imperium*. Sensitive to the re-configuration of the grand theme of *Britannia* following 1603, Owen, like Horace and Virgil after Actium, offers a poetic reappraisal of what can be salvaged from his personal history at the birth of the unprecedented vision of tri-national union, ensuring the survival of the former to the enrichment of the latter. Allusions to Tacitus' account of the Roman conquest of North Wales and to the direct derivation of the island's Welsh name from Latin call to mind a more distant *Britannia*, the unified Roman province, invoked as an imperfect model of what is now fully realized in the evolving historical process. As this is a recurring theme in all Owen's collections, we can judge the extent to which he re-ordered his personal priorities to meet the challenge. Essential aspects of the historical local culture like religion and family loyalty were abandoned; the new religion was the national church, the new family the emerging élite circling around the unifying national symbol of the Scottish–English king. Local language and history still had a role in this re-modelled perspective, and were in any case essential if the concept of a true union of parts was to prevail over that of the conquest by one of all the rest.[49] Latin would serve to express this single national culture for the multilingual local regions, appropriately drawing on an ancient thread in the heritage of each and connecting the whole with the common inheritance of Europe.

This third book of the 1606 collection is unusual in that so many of its 208 poems deal with elevated themes of philosophy and religion,[50] but like the earlier books as well, it wittily enlists their dedicatee, Lady Mary Neville, daughter of the earl of Dorset, to serve the national cause. Once the *onus* of her pregnant mother, Lady Mary is now the family's *honos* (3.2), the reference to her birth opening the way to the Union of the Kingdoms being presented as Elizabeth's true offspring, as if the old queen's physical virginity had been preserved to enable her to give eventual birth to the United Kingdom.[51] The new age is hailed with verbal echoes of Virgil's fourth *Eclogue* (3.6), a note explaining this new *aurea aetas* as the child of James's Scottish ancestry in alliance with the Welsh Tudor family of Henry VII. This genealogical strategy directs the course of the underlying narrative: providence is bringing together Scots, Welsh, and English, Stuarts and Tudors, James, Elizabeth, and Owen himself as threads in the single tapestry of British history, and then giving his dedicatee Lady Mary Neville, who is herself, in a curious parallel, the union of three goddesses in one body,[52] a place of

---

[49] Especially as an alternative picture might present James VI (and his 'martyred' mother!) as having ultimately prevailed over a hated English rival by effortlessly inheriting her hard-won achievements. It was the Civil War of the 1640s, with its military triumph of the English, which displaced the model Owen and others were promoting at the start of the century.

[50] No doubt a tribute to the famed personal piety of the dedicatee, Lady Mary Neville.

[51] 3.4, dated to 1602: *Scotia nobiscum gentem concrescit in unam* / ... *Tuque* [sc. Elizabetha] *magis felix non pariendo Parens.*

[52] Cf. (1606) 1.4 ... *corpus / Intrarunt Pallas, Iuno Venusque tuum* ... *Tres nam virtutes te repperiuntur in una* ....

honour in the overall design. The note to 3.6 in effect gives the stage-directions for this pageant: James's coming south unites the kingdoms of Britain, a country deriving its name and *indivisum . . . diadema* from Brutus (3.6.2; Owen had not forgotten his Geoffrey of Monmouth);[53] since Henry VII's *avus* came from North Wales, the Tudor dynasty also began auspiciously with a journey south, and since, moreover, his name was Owain/Owen, the poet can claim an incidental role for himself in this heaven-sent series of coincidences: *omne bonum nobis ex Aquilone venit* (3.6.6). Such is the *honos* of which the dedicatee is now the fortunate beneficiary.

After a suitably elevating sequence of short religious pieces, this opening theme resumes when the impressive eight couplets of 3.39 celebrate the providential creation of the *tergeminum imperium*, and again at the book's climax (3.201, 202) when an opportunity to bring Brutus back to mind is provided by the Gunpowder Plot. The plotters are depicted as trying to reduce London to ashes, as the Greeks did Troy, and so create a *nova Troia* in Britain, the achievement which, in a very different sense, Geoffrey of Monmouth's opening pages had ascribed to Brutus! Though published in the year following the fateful November, Owen's Gunpowder poems are, to our surprise today, less venomous and embittered than Milton's and interestingly do not link the plot to the Roman Catholic community in particular. The emphasis lies firmly on the success of the new kingdom in triumphing over its enemies in general, as Zeus did over the Giants.[54]

The dedicatory poems to Lady Mary Neville which open each book of the 1606 collection are not the only means by which Owen honours her. Scattered through the books are verses to her two children, Thomas and Cecily, and Richard Sacville, earl of Dorset, and his brother, Edward.[55] More importantly for the Dorsets, the core of this whole collection (2.15–32) is a sequence honouring the king (15), the secretary of state (17), the lord chancellor (19), William Cecil (21–2, by name), and the bishops of London (23) and Winchester (25, now Thomas Bilson). The status and honour of a dedicatee are enhanced when the intended recipients can be seen in the company they would most like to keep, while the author can expect the same device to attract even more eminent dedicatees for the future. The use of Latin offers them an extension of their name and reputation on the Continent, which in part explains Owen's wish to connect with a wider European culture. There

[53] For the significance of the 'Brutus' myth see Kendrick, *British Antiquity*, 7–12 and 34–44 for the manufacturing of a British Tudor ancestry.

[54] The Gigantomachy myth had also been central to Virgil's portrayal of the new Augustan age of peace, security and national unity; see P. R. Hardie, *Virgil's Aeneid, Cosmos and Imperium* (Oxford, 1986), 85–156. Like the Giants, Owen's plotters are trying to pile Pelion on Ossa (3.201.3). For the *nova Troia* and its attempted incineration see 3.202.1–2.

[55] Thomas and Cecily are carefully positioned; together at the start (1.6, 1.7), Cecily then joins her mother at the opening of the third book (3.10) while Owen reserves Thomas, *optimae spei puerum*, until the very end (3.205), where he can inaugurate the next generation. Richard, 2.20; Edward appears in the 1612 collection (2.37) on his return from abroad.

are verses on Scaliger, playfully alluding to the great *Emendatio Temporum* under the invocation *O Tempora! O Mores!* (1.16), and on other scholars and academic matters which are unlikely to have had immediate appeal for Lady Mary Neville and the Dorsets.[56] Most distinctive in this connection are the poems on that *litterateur* of European reputation Sir Philip Sidney (2.28), his daughter (31), and his *Arcadia* (67). The three couplets of this last poem reveal Owen's well-practised procedure: the first recalls the alleged story that Sidney had wanted *Arcadia* to be burnt, the second wittily relates this to the familiar amatory conceit of the flames of love (*Si meruit mortem, quia flammam accendit amoris, /Mergi, non uri, debuit iste liber*), the third broadens this destruction–survival motif to make a more conventional compliment to the author (. . . *nulla/Debuit ingenium morte perire tuum*). As so often with the meta-physical poets, the conceit is the pearl in the oyster. The artistry on display throughout the collection marries the witty conceits, verbal dexterity, and ludic name-play familiar from contemporary English verse[57] to the themes and targets of Erasmian satire, a focus which explains why, in the year follow-ing the Gunpowder Plot, anti-Catholic poems are still restricted to the old medieval and Erasmian targets of simony and abuses of papal power and clerical celibacy; and it is noticeable that Owen balances these with attacks on the ministers of Geneva for hypocrisy.[58]

The success of the first collection can be judged from the fact that the *Liber Singularis* of the following year, containing more poems than any other individual book, carried a dedication to Lady Arabella Stuart and so brought Owen into the royal circle.[59] In 1612 Owen reached his apogee, with the honour of offering dedications to the (doomed) brothers, Henry, prince of Wales and Charles, duke of York, and the extent of his connections at court is now evident from the presence in these three books of verses to Anne of Denmark, James's queen (3.10), Sir Robert Carey (or Ker, 18), Sir Henry Wotton (36), and the princes' tutors Sir James Fullerton (22) and Thomas Moray (26). Henry receives the first two books, Charles the third, an arrange-ment which should suggest in itself that the design of the volume as a whole is carefully calculated. Why three books of roughly equal length rather than two, one for each of the princes, with the first recognizing Henry's priority by its position and greater number of poems? This was the second tripartite collection, and a third, with three dedicatees, would follow in 1613. The recurring structure illustrates the dominant political theme: as each of the

---

[56] 1.12, 2.46, 118, 155–64, 3.191.

[57] Word-play, anagrams, etc.: 1, 44, 53, 59, 79, 90, 118, 131, 2.38, 59, and 110 (unusually on Greek words), 99, 101, and 115 (Latin–English pun on *plaga*), 119, 135, and 152 (*Tho. Morus moriens*), 156, 3.2, 25, 46, 85, 126, and 158 (also Greek). One of the very few Welsh examples is the proverbial game in 1.132 (cf. 3.39), where *nostrum* in line 4 may be taken to confirm Owen's bachelor status.

[58] For the balanced approach see 1.41, 51 and (1607) 24–5.

[59] Note the graceful pun on her name in the dedication (1, line 5) and the confirmation of the patron-client relationship in the concluding compliment (276).

three books contributes its own qualities to the greater distinction and success of the whole, so the new *tergeminum imperium* will succeed by drawing on the genius and resources of each of the peoples now united in the one kingdom.

Symbolic design is one of the most familiar of the calculated effects to be expected from 'metaphysical' artistry. It is therefore especially appropriate that the third book of the third published collection, dedicated to the artistic, refined, and highly cultured Prince Charles, should offer much of Owen's most individual and characteristic work, closely relating him to the contemporary vernacular practice. Puns, allusion, name-play, and anagrams reveal Owen's unparalleled confidence in his verbal ingenuity. On Erasmus: . . . *Eras mus: / Si sum mus, ego te iudice summus ero* (34; cf. 54 in the first book for a rather laboured piece on More); to someone recommending charitable giving: *Qui dare mi suadet pauperibus, sua det* (19); to become a *novus homo*: . . . *de pelle tua depelle vetustum, / De cute peccati decute triste iugum* (13); under a quotation of the opening words of Pindar's first Olympian Ode: *Unde renascuntur mortaes 'unda' vocatur; / A qua nascuntur cuncta, vocatur 'aqua'* (78, with the Greek theme extended to include baptism!); the conversion of St Paul converts *Saulus* into *Salvus*, Greek *phaulos* (base) into *Paulos* (84). Arithmetical games flatter the young dedicatee's attainments (42, 79, 104, 120, cf. 51 in the first book). Other games include tricks with *navis/avis* (25), *sanguis/anguis* (29), *mens/mons* (48), *humanum/humandum* (69), but is to the anagram that Owen here resorts most frequently: *datur/durat* (7), *opto/poto* (14), *uberiora/breviora* (48, a neat Callimachean pair in a poem which also gives us the jingle . . . *montisque cacumen mentis acumen*), *munera/numera* (73), *unda/nuda* (111,113), *terra/errat* (52), *clines/cliens* (54), *verbis/ubi res* (31), and even *patiens/at in spe* (56).[60]

It is in the context of the experimental poetry workshops of later Elizabethan and early Jacobean England that Owen's art can best be understood and receive the recognition it deserves. Both Latin and vernacular verse here shared many of the same techniques and applied them to similar topics. Owen stood out because his exclusive concentration on Latin gave him a voice in the European Protestant cultural mainstream, with which his patrons were obviously keen to be associated by name. The sharing of these patrons and high-placed friends shows the extent to which the circles of Owen and Donne continued to intersect with each other, even when both poets had left Oxford. Sir Thomas Egerton, who had launched Donne's secular career by getting him a seat in Parliament and whose son was Donne's regular companion in the 1590s,[61] was honoured with a lavishly

---

[60] The anagrams, of course, are only visual; no account is taken of vowel quantity.

[61] On the elder Egerton (Lord Keeper), see Bald, *John Donne*, 93–103; on Parliament, 114–16; on the younger Egerton, who died in 1599, and his friendship with Donne, 93.

complimentary pair of couplets from Owen in 1607.[62] The previous year, Sir Henry Goodyer, Donne's great 'Court friend',[63] received from Owen a *consolatio* on the death of his wife,[64] and among the higher nobility we find the two poets sharing the patronage of Richard Sackville, third earl of Dorset, his brother Edward, the fourth earl, and Robert Ker, earl of Somerset.[65] Most revealing of all is the poem which shows us Owen's connection with Donne's long-standing and intimate friend Henry Wotton.[66]

These were among the social elite who invested their hopes and resources in the Union and the new reign, and a part of Owen's appeal for them was no doubt his ability to articulate so effectively the concept of the Union as a *tergeminum imperium*, a coming together of three partners, as it was widely seen at its inception. His youth at Plas Du continued to influence him here, if only by reminding him that, whatever had of necessity to be abandoned, much needed to be salvaged and given new vigour if the traditional local cultures were to mix on equal terms and form a new national one. Detachment from the limiting perspective of the purely local was an essential first step, which we have seen Owen take early in the Oxford years, before a pragmatic and rational evaluation of his regional heritage could contribute to the vision of a new *patria*. We may therefore sense more than the usual ludic dexterity beneath the surface here:

> Illa mihi patria est ubi pascor, non ubi nascor;
> illa ubi sum notus, non ubi natus eram.[67]

The vision of Owen and his friends was not to be realized. Within a century of his death, a disastrous civil war and the expulsion of the Stuarts helped to transform their hopes for the new Union into a cultural and administrative hegemony. Only very recently has any radical shift in this bias begun to restore something of the balanced partnership Owen proclaimed the Union to be. This in itself would not have surprised a poet whose most famous line (not, in fact, his own)[68] announced that history, like humanity, is in constant flux. It should, however, encourage us to read his poetic legacy as a fresh and useful contribution to the current realignment of our historical perspectives.

University of Wales, Swansea

---

[62] (1607) 133, in combination with his son-in-law, Sir Francis Leigh of Cheshire (Bald, *John Donne*, 96).

[63] Bald, *John Donne*, 170, but see *passim* 163–71 for Donne's close ties with Goodyer.

[64] In 1606, but published in (1607) 74; cf. (1606) 2.33.

[65] Richard, (1606) 2.20 (Bald, *John Donne*, 324); Edward, (1612) 2.37 (Bald, *John Donne*, 455); Robert, (1612) 3.18 (Bald, *John Donne*, 271–315 *passim*).

[66] (1612) 3.36; on Donne's special intimacy with Wotton, Bald, *John Donne*, 119–24.

[67] (1612) 3.100, lines 3–4; a late poem given added significance by the superscription.

[68] *Tempora mutantur, nos et mutamur in illis* is a sixteenth-century maxim quoted by Owen in (1613) 1.58 and commented on in the ensuing pentameter.

3

The poetic debate of Edmwnd Prys and Wiliam Cynwal

GRUFFYDD ALED WILLIAMS

In Wales, the true remnant of the ancient Britons, as there are good authorities to show the long time they had poets, which they called *bards*, so through all the conquests of Romans, Saxons, Danes, and Normans . . . yet do their poets even to this day last; so as it is not more notable in soon beginning than in long continuing.[1]

In this brief tribute by Sir Philip Sidney in his *Apology for Poetry*, written in the early 1580s, the hidden world (to outside eyes) of the Welsh poetic tradition momentarily intruded into the world of Renaissance poetics. During these very years in Wales itself, these same two worlds were to come together in a rather more confrontational fashion. I refer to the celebrated poetic debate – the longest of its kind in Welsh literary history, comprising a total of fifty-four poems, amounting to some five and a half thousand lines exchanged over seven years between 1581 and 1588 – in which the participants were the humanist Edmwnd Prys, archdeacon of Merioneth, and the professional poet Wiliam Cynwal.[2]

To the debate the two protagonists brought with them intellectual baggage and preconceptions derived from their very different training and backgrounds. Prys, a native of Llanrwst in Denbighshire and a kinsman of the humanist William Salesbury, entered St John's College, Cambridge in 1565.[3] In this nursery of the 'new learning' – founded by John Fisher, bishop of Rochester, and where Sir John Cheke and Roger Ascham had served as fellows – he spent the best part of twelve years, graduating B.A. in 1568 and M.A. in 1571.[4] He was elected fellow of the college in 1570, college preacher in 1574, and chaplain in 1575;[5] in 1575–6 he also served as university

---

[1] Sir Philip Sidney, *An Apology for Poetry or The Defence of Poesy*, ed. Geoffrey Shepherd (London and Edinburgh, 1965), 98.

[2] Gruffydd Aled Williams (ed.), *Ymryson Edmwnd Prys a Wiliam Cynwal* (Cardiff, 1986). All references are to this edition, which is based on Prys's holograph copy of the debate in National Library of Wales Llanstephan MS 43. References generally cite poem and line numbers.

[3] John Venn and J. A. Venn, *The Book of Matriculations and Degrees* (Cambridge, 1913), 473, 542.

[4] *Ibid.*

[5] T. Baker, *History of St. John's College*, ed. J. E. B. Mayor (2 vols, Cambridge, 1869), I, 289, 333 records his election as fellow and college preacher. His election as chaplain *pro fundatrice* is recorded in the college's accounts for 1575–6 (St John's College Archives, rental 1575–99).

preacher. Prys's education at St John's – where his contemporaries included
Andrew Downes, later regius professor of Greek, and the Welshmen William
Morgan, translator of the Bible into Welsh, Richard Vaughan, later bishop of
London, and Hugh Broughton, the Hebrew scholar – provided him with a rich
endowment of humanist and theological learning. This would have embraced,
among other things, considerable linguistic learning, a source of pride for
Prys, who boasted in his debate with Cynwal of his acquaintance with poetry in
eight languages.[6] This suggests that apart from the three classical languages,
his native Welsh, and acquired English, it is likely that he had some knowledge
of modern continental vernaculars. His university contemporary Gabriel
Harvey mentions the vogue of French and Italian among the Cambridge
men of his day.[7] Prys's friend William Morgan is credited with a knowledge
of French,[8] and it may be significant that during the two Welshmen's time at
St John's the Frenchman Antoine Chevallier – said to have been French tutor
to Princess Elizabeth – served as Hebrew lecturer there.[9]

Despite being appointed rector of Ffestiniog and Maentwrog in Merioneth
in 1573 and later appointments in 1576 as rector of Ludlow and archdeacon
of Merioneth, evidence suggests that Prys was partly resident at Cambridge
until mid-1577.[10] Having relinquished his Ludlow living in 1579, he settled
in Maentwrog, his home for the remainder of his life. Here, combining his
clerical duties with the life of a well-to-do country gentleman and justice of
the peace, he also found time to indulge in his passion for Welsh poetry. The
quality of his output, which consisted of both moral and divine verse, as well
as occasional poetry of various kinds (including poetic debates with three
other poets apart from Cynwal, all of lesser extent and import), places him
in the highest rank of Welsh poets of the day. His masterpiece, a metrical
version of the Psalms – commended for both its sustained poetic force and
copiousness of Welsh diction – was composed in old age, being published as
an appendix to the 1621 Book of Common Prayer.[11] Significantly, in view of
his humanist background, he did not confine his poetic efforts to Welsh. His
manuscript poems include examples of the Welsh *englyn* metre written in

[6] Williams, *Ymryson*, 17.75–6. Cynwal also refers to Prys's knowledge of eight languages, *ibid.* 19.15.
[7] *Three Proper, and Wittie, Familiar Letters* (London, 1580); see *The Poetical Works of Edmund Spenser*, ed.
J. C. Smith and E. De Selincourt (London, 1912), 621.
[8] R. Geraint Gruffydd, 'William Morgan', in Geraint Bowen (ed.), *Y Traddodiad Rhyddiaith* (Llandysul,
1970), 162; *idem*, *'The Translating of the Bible into the Welsh Tongue' by William Morgan in 1588* (London, 1988),
33.
[9] Chevallier was Hebrew lecturer at the college 1569–72 (St John's College Archives, rentals 1555–74).
See further my note 'William Morgan ac Edmwnd Prys yng Nghaer-grawnt', *The Bulletin of the Board of Celtic
Studies*, XXIX (1980–2), 298–300.
[10] He received his stipend as fellow and preacher at St Johns for the first two quarters of the 1576–7
financial year (St John's College Archives, rentals 1575–99). The college statutes prohibited preachers from
being absent for more than eight weeks a year. For the details of Prys's clerical career see A. Owen Evans,
'Edmund Prys: archdeacon of Merioneth, priest, preacher, poet', *Transactions of the Honourable Society of
Cymmrodorion* (1922–3), 126–34.
[11] Edmwnd Prys, *Llyfr y Psalmau, wedi eu cyfieithu, a'i cyfansoddi ar fesur cerdd, yn Gymraeg* (London, 1621).

Latin, and in 1621 a Latin hexameter poem of his praising the author and his work was prefaced to Dr John Davies of Mallwyd's Welsh grammar, *Antiquae Linguae Britannicae . . . Rudimenta.*[12]

Prys's adversary, Wiliam Cynwal, was the product of native bardic education.[13] It was customary for aspiring poets to learn their art from a bardic teacher; like many of the leading professional poets of Elizabethan Wales, Cynwal had been taught by Gruffudd Hiraethog, the foremost bardic teacher of his day. Welsh bardic education had its own hierarchy of qualifications; Cynwal had progressed within this system, having been awarded the second highest degree of *disgybl pencerddaidd* at the Caerwys eisteddfod of 1567, later gaining the premier degree of *pencerdd* at a nuptial feast, a regular setting for bardic graduation. Cynwal was proficient in all branches of traditional bardic learning. Like his teacher Gruffudd Hiraethog, he was particularly expert in genealogy and heraldry, his learning in these fields being amply demonstrated in his surviving genealogical and heraldic manuscripts, and in extensive references in his poetry. His manuscripts of *Brut y Tywysogion* and *Brut y Brenhinedd*, the Welsh translation of Geoffrey of Monmouth's *Historia Regum Britanniae*, testify to his familiarity with historical and pseudo-historical lore, and two separate versions of the Welsh bardic grammar which he compiled also survive in manuscript. His poetic output during a career spanning just under a quarter of a century was prolific: over 300 substantial poems (*cywyddau* and *awdlau*) by him have survived, as well as almost 500 quatrains (*englynion*).[14] The bulk of his output, as befitted a professional poet, consisted of eulogies and elegies to patrons – almost exclusively gentry and clergy from north Wales – but love poetry and moral and religious verse were also well represented in his work. He was a competent but rather pedestrian poet whose work was thoroughly traditional, hardly ever deviating from the well-worn paradigms of bardic verse, the only innovative feature found in his work being the occasional metrical experimentation of some of his odes. Unlike some of his professional Welsh bardic contemporaries, Cynwal – who lived in the remote upland parish of Ysbyty Ifan, Denbighshire – is not known to have travelled outside Wales and its borderlands, and his cultural horizons may have been more circumscribed than those of some of his fellows.[15] It may be significant that in an elegy to the humanist Humphrey Lhuyd of

---

[12] Prys, *Llyfr y Psalmau*, d4ʳ. See further Ceri Davies, 'Cerddi Rhagymadroddol Lladin a Llyfrau'r Dyneiddwyr Cymreig', *Llên Cymru*, 23 (2000), 106–8.

[13] Cynwal's career and poetry are discussed by Enid Roberts, 'Wiliam Cynwal', *Denbighshire Historical Society Transactions*, 12 (1963), 51–85, Rhiannon Williams, 'Wiliam Cynwal', *Llên Cymru*, 8 (1964–5), 197–213; G. P. Jones and R. L. Jones, 'Wiliam Cynwal', *Llên Cymru*, 11 (1970–1), 176–204.

[14] His work has been edited in three University of Wales M.A. theses: Sarah Rhiannon Williams, 'Testun beirniadol o gasgliad Llawysgrif Mostyn 111 o waith Wiliam Cynwal ynghyd â rhagymadrodd, nodiadau a geirfa' (1965), Geraint Percy Jones, 'Astudiaeth destunol o ganu Wiliam Cynwal yn Llawysgrif (Bangor) Mostyn 4' (1969), and Richard Lewis Jones, 'Astudiaeth destunol o awdlau, cywyddau ac englynion gan Wiliam Cynwal' (1969).

[15] A point emphasized by Roberts, 'Wiliam Cynwal', 80–2.

Denbigh – an antiquary and cartographer who had collaborated with Abraham Ortelius – Cynwal ignored Llwyd's wider humanistic learning and was content to commemorate the dead man's proficiency in genealogy and heraldry, branches of learning which were within his ken.[16] It may be that Prys could have found more intellectually alert adversaries among the bardic fraternity; yet Cynwal, by virtue of his bardic standing and acquaintance with the native learned tradition, was not an unworthy representative of the professional poets of his day.

The cultural differences between Prys and Cynwal are clearly illustrated by the references and allusions in the poems they exchanged. Not unexpectedly, in Prys's poems classical references abound. It may be suspected that he sometimes employed these to bemuse Cynwal: in one poem he greets Cynwal as 'a learned Homer' (*Homer hyddysg*)[17] – a complement he would have understood, as he himself later addresses Prys as a 'Homer of learning' (*Homer addysc*)[18] – but other comparisons where he likened Cynwal to the poet Archias, who featured in Cicero's *Pro Archia poeta* and *Epistolae ad Atticum*, and to Cato the Elder, commemorated in the same author's *De Senectute*, would surely have puzzled his adversary![19] Prys's classical references embrace both Greek and Latin authors. There are references derived from Plato's *Hippias minor* and either his *Ion* or *Respublica* (Prys's knowledge of the latter being probably indirect as it reflects the influence of commentators, such as Eusebius, who had equated Plato's Musaeus with Moses).[20] He boasts of his acquaintance with the work of Euclid[21] – a staple ingredient in the sixteenth-century Cambridge mathematical curriculum – and alludes twice to a tale about Lycurgus of Sparta derived from Plutarch's *Moralia*.[22] Not unexpectedly, Latin authors provided Prys with rather more references. Lines which cite Cicero as their source conflate passages from *Pro Archia poeta*, *De Finibus*, and *De Oratore*.[23] Other references derive ultimately and possibly directly from Livy's *Ab Urbe Condita*.[24] He certainly had direct knowledge of Horace's *Ars Poetica*: he quotes from it in a marginal gloss in his holograph copy of the

---

[16] For a text of Cynwal's elegy see R. Geraint Gruffydd, 'Humphrey Llwyd of Denbigh: some documents and a catalogue', *Denbighshire Historical Society Transactions*, 17 (1968), 97–9.

[17] Williams, *Ymryson*, 3.20.

[18] *Ibid.* 10.2.

[19] *Ibid.* 5.2, 9.2.

[20] *Ibid.* 11.48, 25.59–60. The passages in question are *Hippias minor* 364; *Ion* 536B; *Respublica* 363D. On the equation of Musaeus and Moses see Ernst Robert Curtius, *European Literature and the Latin Middle Ages*, trans. Willard R. Trask (London and Henley, 1953), 211; Edgar Wind, *Pagan Mysteries in the Renaissance*, new edn (London, 1968), 278.

[21] Williams, *Ymryson*, 42.56.

[22] *Ibid.* 24.3–6, 42.9–14. The references are based on *Moralia* 3A.

[23] Williams, *Ymryson*, 50.33–42. The relevant passages are *Pro Archia* 1.2 and *De Finibus* 3.19.

[24] Williams, *Ymryson*, 50.45–52. The reference is to the tale of the belly and the body members, *Ab Urbe Condita* 2.32.9–11. Cf. also Plutarch, *Caius Marcius Coriolanus* 6.3–4. It should be noted, however, that the tale was often included in sixteenth-century school books; see T. W. Baldwin, *William Shakspere's Small Latine and Lesse Greeke* (Urbana, 1944), II, 321–2.

debate in Llanstephan MS 43.[25] Another work he quotes in a marginal note
is Ovid's *Fasti*,[26] a work he evidently found more to his taste than other
unnamed works by the poet – probably the *Ars Amatoria* or the *Amores* –
which he condemns on moral grounds elsewhere in the debate.[27] Prys almost
certainly also knew Pliny's *Historia naturalis*, his likely source of knowledge
about the Greek artists Apelles and Zeuxis.[28]

References by Prys to other works are what one might expect from a man
of his training and background. In the forty-seventh poem of the debate he
claims three sources to be supremely authoritative in historical matters: the
Bible, the Church Fathers, and the histories of the ancient world.[29] Biblical
references are frequent in his poems: in discussing 'the sons of God' and
'the daughters of men' of Genesis 6 he cites the Church Fathers as supporting authorities, adopting an interpretation found in the works of St Augustine, Cyril of Alexandria, Chrysostom, and other patristic authors, but which
also occurs in Renaissance biblical commentaries with which he may have
been familiar.[30] Prys's cultural name-dropping – one wonders again what
Cynwal would have made of it – also extended to medieval literature. He
refers not only to Petrarch and Thomas à Kempis, but also to the lesser
known Gunther of Pairis, a twelfth-century Cistercian Latin poet from Alsace
whose *Ligurinus*, an epic based on the history of Frederick Barbarossa, had
been published by Conrad Celtis in 1507.[31] As might be expected, Prys also
drew on near-contemporary works, representing a wide spectrum of literary,
historical, scientific, and theological interest. The most notable example of
this occurs in the twenty-first poem of the debate, which largely consists of
a skilful versification of passages from Erasmus's *Moriae Encomium*.[32] Another
contemporary work on which Prys drew heavily was John Bale's *Scriptorum
Illustrium Maioris Brytanniae . . . Catalogus*, published in Basel in 1557:[33] he

---

[25] The lines quoted (Llanstephan MS 43, 82) are *Ars poetica* 9–10, cf. Williams, *Ymryson*, 24.23–8.
[26] *Fasti* 1.29 (Llanstephan MS 43, 149), cf. Williams, *Ymryson*, 44.89–92.
[27] *Ibid.* 42.42.
[28] *Ibid.* 13.47–56. His reference to Zeuxis (lines 49–56) is fairly detailed, cf. Pliny, *Historia naturalis* 35.65–
6. Apelles (*ibid.* 35.79–97) is merely named.
[29] Williams, *Ymryson*, 47.1–12.
[30] *Ibid.* 47.37–42. Prys equated 'the sons of God' with the descendants of Seth and 'the daughters of men'
with the descendants of Cain. For instances of this interpretation in the works of patristic authors see
Don Cameron Allen, 'Milton and the sons of God', *Modern Language Notes*, LXI (1946), 74–5. On its occurrence
in Renaissance commentaries see Arnold Williams, *The Common Expositor: An Account of the Commentaries on
Genesis, 1527–1633* (Chapel Hill, 1948), 152–3.
[31] Williams, *Ymryson*, 50.19–24. These authors are cited by Prys as examples of clerics who also composed
poetry.
[32] The passages versified by Prys are cited in my notes accompanying Williams, *Ymryson*, poem 21. See also
Ceri Davies, 'Erasmus and Welsh Renaissance learning', *Transactions of the Honourable Society of Cymmrodorion*
(1983), 4. As indicated therein, some of the many proverbs versified by Prys in the debate are found in
Erasmus's *Adagia*.
[33] Williams, *Ymryson*, 27.32–8, 71–80, 43.69–84, and 51.45–58 are passages which are indebted to Bale. Bale
drew extensively on John Leland's *Commentarii de Scriptoribus Britannicis* (*c.* 1540, but not published until
1709). Prys's debt to Bale (and ultimately to Leland) was first demonstrated by G. J. Williams, 'Leland a Bale
a'r Traddodiad Derwyddol', *Llên Cymru*, 4 (1956–7), 21.

eagerly seized upon Bale's fictional claims regarding the scientific learning of early British poets, implying by contrast Cynwal's ignorance of such matters. Prys's own acquaintance with scientific works is reflected in his approbation of Sebastian Münster's popular *Cosmographia Vniversalis* (first published in 1544) as a repository of geographical lore,[34] and in his contrasting condemnatory remark about the medieval Alphonsine astronomical tables,[35] which shows him to be aware of their displacement by the *Tabulae Prutenicae* (1551) of Erasmus Reinhold based on the Copernican system. His reading in contemporary theology is reflected in a marginal reference he makes to the Dutch Protestant theologian Andreas Hyperius, whose *Methodi Theologiae* he draws upon to repudiate the tale of Merlin's generation by an incubus.[36]

Works such as I have cited – largely the garnered fruits of his cosmopolitan humanist education – did not constitute the whole of Prys's cultural endowment. In the twenty-fourth poem of the debate he lists the 'excellent men, ancient authors' (*Hynod wŷr, hen awdvriaid*) who were his poetic mentors: the names of Homer, Horace, and Ovid are not unexpected, but Prys also cites Guto'r Glyn and Tudur Aled, two of the poetic greats of late medieval Wales.[37] The list is significant in indicating the hybrid nature of Prys's cultural inheritance. Not only does he compare Cynwal to Homer and Archias, but he also compares him to Tydain Tad Awen, Adda Fras, and Cynddelw,[38] celebrated figures in the Welsh poetic tradition (it is likely that there was a tongue-in-cheek element in the hyperbole of all these comparisons!). Other names of note in Welsh tradition cited by him are Taliesin and the two Merlins,[39] a trio considered at the time to be the founding fathers of native poesy. In response to Cynwal's criticism that he did not possess a bardic degree he could cite examples of Welsh amateur poets of previous generations as well as of his own who were similarly without formal qualifications;[40] elsewhere he provided another list of former Welsh poets who had been

---

[34] Williams, *Ymryson*, 42.55. Prys also refers to Münster (and to another Renaissance cosmographer, Oronce Finé) in a poem to Sir John Wynn the younger of Gwydir, John Wyn Roberts, 'Edmwnd Prys: Hanes ei Fywyd a Chasgliad o'i Weithiau' [University of Wales M.A. thesis, 1938], xci.25–30.

[35] Williams, *Ymryson*, 44.85–8.

[36] *Ibid.* 9.21–36. The marginal note in Llanstephan MS 43, 30, opposite these lines cites 'Andr. Hipperius de succubis et incubis'. The *Methodi Theologiae* was first published (date unknown) in Marburg, where Hyperius (1511–64) was professor of theology. I have seen references to three editions of the work published in Basel (1567, 1568, 1574). The lines in question by Prys correspond to passages in the 1574 Basel edition, 304–5.

[37] These lines do not occur in Llanstephan MS 43 on which my edited text of the debate is based, being found in three manuscripts only (the earliest being BL Additional MS 31056) which preserve the β version of the debate (Williams, *Ymryson*, lii–lxi). The β version pre-dates Prys's revised version in Llanstephan MS 43. The lines are printed with the textual variants in Williams, *Ymryson*, 110.

[38] Williams, *Ymryson*, 1.10, 13, 5.17.

[39] *Ibid.* 9.17–18, 26.23–4, 27.27–30, 51.51–4. The two Merlins were Merlin Ambrosius (the Merlin of Geoffrey of Monmouth's *Historia Regum Britanniae*) and Merlin Sylvester (the Merlin of antecedent Welsh tradition).

[40] Williams, *Ymryson*, 48.59–68.

clerics like himself.[41] But Prys's knowledge of the Welsh literary tradition allowed him to do much more than indulge in mere name-dropping. His references to earlier poetic debates, that between Dafydd ap Gwilym and Gruffudd Gryg in the fourteenth-century, and those between Rhys Goch Eryri and Llywelyn ap y Moel and Rhys Goch Eryri and Siôn Cent a few decades later,[42] indicate a direct acquaintance with their texts; it is likely that he had access to manuscript copies of these earlier bardic clashes. In defending technical features of his verse criticized by Cynwal – minutiae related to *cynghanedd* – he could cite the usage of the fifteenth-century masters Dafydd ab Edmwnd, Guto'r Glyn, and Tudur Aled.[43] Prys may have drunk deep from the fountains of Renaissance learning; it cannot be doubted, however, that he was also intimately acquainted with the literary tradition of Wales, in particular its rich bardic heritage.

Cynwal's range of reference is altogether more limited than that of Prys, and not only because he contributed only half as many poems to the debate. It is true that Cynwal complements his adversary as a veritable Gregory, Augustine, and Jerome,[44] but these had long been stock comparisons in poems addressed by Welsh poets to clerics. Further examples in which he addresses Prys as both a Plato and a Homer are similarly conventional and in no way indicate direct acquaintance with classical literature.[45] Where Cynwal's references are at all fleshed out they are generally of three distinct kinds. First, there is evidence of his familiarity with lore deriving from scripture, and in some cases developed in later tradition. In recounting the story of ancient human colonization, he mentions both Adam and Noah and their sons, and details the post-diluvial division of the world.[46] (Claiming, in accordance with medieval tradition, that Shem had obtained Asia, Ham Africa, and Japheth Europe, he allowed his adversary to impute his geographical obscurantism, Prys mischievously inquiring who then had obtained America![47]) Secondly, there are references deriving from Welsh historical tradition, sometimes relating to bardic lore – like Prys, he refers to Taliesin and the two Merlins – but principally history as narrated by Geoffrey of Monmouth,[48] a Welsh version of whose *Brut* occurs in one of Cynwal's manuscripts. (Cynwal's naive repetition of Geoffrey's tale that Merlin was begotten by an incubus attracted the merciless ridicule of Prys, who scathingly dismissed it as superstition and heresy.[49]) Thirdly, there are references derived from medieval texts in international circulation, notably the story of

[41] *Ibid.* 50.25–30.
[42] *Ibid.* C (Prys's letter to Cynwal).7–8, 15.45–8, 25.87–90, 44 *passim.*
[43] *Ibid.* 29.41–50.
[44] *Ibid.* 4.30, 34, 88.
[45] *Ibid.* 4.41, 10.2.
[46] *Ibid.* 37.41–68.
[47] *Ibid.* 46.23–8.
[48] *Ibid.* 8.45–50, 12.59, 20.85, 30.76.
[49] *Ibid.* 9.19–36, 26.41–74, 43.35–86; also C (Prys's letter).27–30.

the mythical priest-king Prester John,[50] and the Travels of Sir John Mandeville;[51] the 'Letter of Prester John' was available to Cynwal in Welsh, and Mandeville's Travels, though not translated until 1586, had been known to Welsh poets since the fifteenth century. It will be seen that Cynwal's cultural world, as revealed in his range of references, was very different from that of Prys. Lacking the breadth which derived from Prys's linguistic attainments – Cynwal knew Welsh and some English, but no other language – his world was inevitably more circumscribed; it was also, in essence, a medieval world – hardly distinguishable from that of his fifteenth-century bardic predecessors – and one where the 'new learning', which Prys and his like had imbibed through their university training, was almost entirely beyond its horizons.

A brief word about the externals of the debate is in order here. It was initially a dispute about a yew bow from Antwerp, a gift to Cynwal from a brother of Sir Richard Clough, Sir Thomas Gresham's agent in that city. Cynwal promised to lend the bow to one of Prys's neighbours, on condition that Prys wrote a poem requesting it.[52] Prys wrote his poem, but had to wait two years for a reply, a poem from Cynwal accompanied by a letter explaining that he had given the bow to Dr Ellis Price, one of his leading patrons. From such beginnings did the exchange develop, its initial cause being soon forgotten. Seven poems by each poet exchanged alternatively were followed by two series of three poems each, then by two further series of nine each. Having written a letter to Cynwal enlarging upon some of the points at issue, Prys embarked on a series of twenty-seven poems, cut short after he had written sixteen by news of Cynwal's death. Prys then concluded matters by writing an elegy for him, charitably adopting the principle *de mortuis nil nisi bonum.*

Like other Welsh poetic debates, that between Prys and Cynwal contains some minor backbiting, such as Prys's claim that Cynwal had used English words,[53] and charges by both poets that the other employed faulty *cynghanedd.*[54] But it was larger issues which predominated, and it is on these I shall concentrate in the remainder of this article. Inevitably the main focus will be on Prys: he was very much the leading protagonist, not only the author of most of the poems, but also the one who dictated the terms of the debate, who energetically sought to lead the discussion in new directions. Faced with such a redoubtable adversary, Cynwal gives an impression of relative passivity, generally confining himself to merely responding to Prys's

[50] *Ibid.* 6.2, 8.37–44.
[51] *Ibid.* 20.41–4, 33.17–32. Interestingly, Cynwal (33.31–2) refers to Mandeville's Travels as a printed work; he may have been familiar with one of Thomas East's English editions (1568, 1582).
[52] The circumstances are outlined in a prose preface to the debate in Llanstephan MS 43, 2; see Williams, *Ymryson,* 1–2.
[53] *Ibid.* 5.57–62; C (Prys's letter).41–9.
[54] *Ibid.* 29.37–52, C (Prys's letter).50–5, 94–9. *Cynghanedd* was the strict system of consonance, sometimes combined with internal rhyme, used in Welsh bardic poetry. The debate was conducted entirely in the *cywydd* metre in which the use of *cynghanedd* was mandatory.

promptings and adopting a rather defensive stance in the face of his critical onslaughts.

During the Renaissance, as in classical and medieval times, the application of moral yardsticks to literature was commonplace. It is, therefore, not surprising that one of the two main charges levelled by Prys against Cynwal – and implicitly against other professional poets – was of a moral nature, namely the charge of mendacity. The charge was first raised in the context of discussing *awen*, or poetic inspiration. Unlike Cynwal, who posited the existence of a single, divinely inspired muse,[55] Prys argued for the existence of two contrasting muses; he owed the concept to an earlier scourge of the professional bards, the fifteenth-century poet Siôn Cent, whose verse at one point he urged Cynwal to consult.[56] The first of Prys's two muses was the free muse, manifested in the inspiration granted to Adam in the Vale of Ebron, and exemplified in biblical narrative in the powers bestowed on Moses' seventy elders of Israel, on Saul's messengers before Samuel at Ramah, and upon the disciples at Pentecost.[57] This muse, Prys asserted, was not bestowed by dubious agencies such as a potion from a witch's cauldron – a reference to the cauldron of Ceridwen in the legend of Taliesin – or the ingestion of toadstools or any mantic rite, neither did it derive from the frenzy associated with *furor poeticus*.[58] Untainted by such origins, poetry inspired by the free muse was characterized by its adherence to truth, and, said Prys pointedly, was not granted to any professional poet.[59] In contrast to this beneficent free muse, Prys posited also a second muse, the enslaved muse (*yr awen gaeth*), which lacked truth and which derived, he said, from 'the ancient Serpent'.[60] This, he claimed, was the muse of Merlin and Taliesin, the founding fathers of Welsh bardism, a muse which by dint of its mendacity was contrary to Christian religion.[61] Prys's debt to Siôn Cent, who had claimed an infernal origin for the muse of the professional poets, is again apparent.

Having proposed a link between the bardic muse and mendacity in general terms, Prys proceeded to lay specific charges of mendacity against Cynwal (these again had correspondences in Siôn Cent's earlier attack on professional poets). The charges he made were the attribution of false pedigrees and coats-of-arms, and the lying praise of worthless patrons for their bravery, generosity, justice, and wisdom, virtues which they patently lacked.[62] Given Cynwal's expertise in genealogy and heraldry, it is not surprising that Prys focused his criticism especially on these facets of bardism. Books of

---

[55] *Ibid.* 12.41–4. For the relevant poem by Siôn Cent see Henry Lewis, Thomas Roberts and Ifor Williams (eds), *Cywyddau Iolo Goch ac Eraill*, 2nd edn (Cardiff, 1937), LX.
[56] Williams, *Ymryson*, 15.47–8.
[57] *Ibid.* 25.101–30. The relevant Biblical references are Num. 11.11–25; 1 Sam. 19.18–24 and Acts 2.
[58] Williams, *Ymryson*, 25.51–8.
[59] *Ibid.* 25.143–4.
[60] *Ibid.* 26.10.
[61] *Ibid.* 26.21–8.
[62] *Ibid.* 26. 75–92.

pedigrees and painted heraldic rolls, he asserted in the forty-ninth poem of
the debate, were full of lies, a charge elaborated at length by claims that
Cynwal had attributed noble status to artisans, bondsmen, and concubines.[63]
At the close of the poem, the criticism is applied more widely: among the
thousands who purchased eulogies, claimed Prys, rare indeed were the buyers
of truth (*Yn brin iawn a bryno wîr*)![64] It is apparent that the criticism aimed
ostensibly at Cynwal had others within its sights, being aimed – like Siôn
Cent's earlier strictures – at professional poets in general and at the eulogistic tradition which was their stock in trade.

The association of poetry with mendacity had ancient roots: a long line of
authors ranging from Plato to St Augustine, not to mention numerous later
medieval moralists, would have agreed with Prys. What one critic, Robert J.
Clements,[65] has described as 'a mediaeval Christian conviction' that poetry
was wed to falsehood was certainly current in Wales: in this context, Prys's
immediate model, Siôn Cent, may have had a soulmate in a late thirteenth-
century bishop of St Asaph, Anian II, said to have been the author of a tract
entitled *Commentum in Fabulas Poetarum.*[66] Yet, we are concerned here with
what was not only a medieval phenomenon but also one which was most
definitely widely current in the Renaissance. In his *De incertitudine & Vanitate
scientiarum*, the German humanist Cornelius Agrippa castigated poetry as
'architectrix mendaciorum',[67] whilst Alberico Gentili, George Buchanan, and
J.-C. Scaliger all referred to the commonly held opinion that identified poets
with mendacity.[68] A reflex of this, the notion that mendacity in poetry was
not to be commended, permeated the critical utterings of the Pléiade concerning other writers, classical, medieval, and contemporary:[69] 'tu mentois',
said Ronsard disapprovingly of Pindar.[70] And Edmwnd Prys was not the
only Welsh humanist who accused contemporary poets of lying: the charge
is found also in the works of the grammarians Gruffydd Robert and Siôn
Dafydd Rhys – both of whom had experienced the culture of Renaissance
Italy at first hand[71] – and is levelled too by the Protestant translator Maurice

[63] *Ibid.* 49.57–64; 49.89–98.
[64] *Ibid.* 49.101–4.
[65] *Critical Theory and Practice of the Pléiade* (Cambridge, 1942), 7.
[66] Glanmor Williams, *The Welsh Church from Conquest to Reformation* (Cardiff, 1962), 189.
[67] Published in Cologne (1537), sig. B3.
[68] Quoted by Clements, *Critical Theory*, 10–11.
[69] This phenomenon is discussed with examples in Clements, *Critical Theory*, 13–34.
[70] *Ibid.* 15, where Ronsard's description of Hesiod as 'le vieil Ascréan qui ment' is also quoted.
[71] *Gramadeg Cymraeg gan Gruffydd Robert*, ed. G. J. Williams (Cardiff, 1939), [208]; John David Rhys, *Cambro-brytannicae Cymraecaeve Linguae Institutiones et Rudimenta* (London, 1592), sig. ***1'–***2'. Robert, a Catholic exile who became a canon of Milan and confessor to St Carlo Borromeo, published his Welsh grammar in Milan in separate parts (1567, 1584–); see introduction to Williams, *Gramadeg Cymraeg*. Rhys (variously styled Siôn Dafydd Rhys, John David Rhys, and John Davies) was a tutor in the household of a member of the Gheri family in Pistoia, later graduating in medicine at Siena; he published Welsh, Latin, and Greek grammars, and a treatise on Italian pronunciation. On his career see R. Geraint Gruffydd, 'The life of Dr. John Davies of Brecon (Siôn Dafydd Rhys)', The Cecil Williams Memorial Lecture, 1971, *Transactions of the Honourable Society of Cymmrodorion* (1971), 175–90; *idem*, 'Dr John Davies, "the old man of Brecknock"', *Archaeologia Cambrensis*, CXLI (1992), 1–13.

Kyffin.[72] Notwithstanding the medieval and earlier antecedents of the criticism he levelled against Cynwal, Prys was also applying a criterion which was commonplace in the literary culture of his day.[73] Oblivious to more sophisticated literary attitudes to poetic veracity deriving from Aristotle's contention that poetry dealt with ideal truth rather than actual fact – the *Poetics* were little known in England before the 1580s – Prys, considered in an European context, could justly be included among those who have been described as 'philosophically more naïve writers who seemingly identified truth only with particular fact'.[74]

Apart from the mendacity of Cynwal's praise poems, Prys also charged him with another type of untruth, the kind exemplified by the tales he relates in the debate about Merlin and Sir John Mandeville.[75] Other 'enlightened' Tudor writers – Leland, Bale, and Humphrey Llwyd – had rejected Geoffrey of Monmouth's tale of Merlin's generation by an incubus.[76] Apart from its inherent improbability, Prys also had a theological objection to this tale: he refers to Andreas Hyperius's *Methodi Theologiae*, where it is discussed, asserting, like Hyperius, that Christ alone had been born of the Spirit.[77] There is no doubt that Prys's Protestantism was a factor in this context. One detects a certain delight in his rational explanation of Merlin's paternity, namely that his mother, a nun, had consorted with a monk;[78] in discussing the same issue later on in the debate, he explicitly warns Cynwal not to corrupt Welsh learning with vain tales derived from 'the old confession'.[79] His Protestantism too may have coloured his attitude to Mandeville's Travels, with their accounts of the saints, crusades, and pilgrimages: Protestant suspicion of such elements in the Travels was the reason why they were so little published in sixteenth-century England and Germany compared to Catholic countries.[80]

---

[72] M. Kyffin, *Deffynniad Ffydd Eglwys Loegr*, ed. W. Prichard Williams (Bangor, 1908), [x].

[73] Despite the religious gulf which separated them, there are parallels between Prys's standpoint and those of Counter-Reformation Italian critics (e.g. Antonio Possevino and Tommaso Campanella) who similarly emphasize the need for *veritas* in poetry; see Bernard Weinberg, *A History of Literary Criticism in the Italian Renaissance* (Chicago, 1961), 307–8, 792–3, 1066–8. One of the works discussed by Weinberg, the *Tractatio de perfectae poëseos ratione* (1576), was attributed to Lorenzo Gambara, but was actually written by Possevino; see Luigi Balsamo, *Church, Censorship and Culture in Early Modern Italy*, ed. Gigliola Fragnito, trans. Adrian Belton (Cambridge, 2001), 54.

[74] Baxter Hathaway, *The Age of Criticism: the Late Renaissance in Italy* (Ithaca, 1962), 163.

[75] Prys attacks Cynwal's observations on Merlin in Williams, *Ymryson*, 9. 19–40; 17.43–4, 26.41–74, C (letter to Cynwal).26–30; 43.23–96 and 49.17–22. Criticism of what Cynwal says about Sir John Mandeville are found *ibid*. 24.13–48 and 42.35–100.

[76] John Leland, *Commentarii de Scriptoribus Britannicis*, ed. Anthony Hall (Oxford, 1709), 42; John Bale, *Scriptorum Illustrium Maioris Brytanniae . . . Catalogus*, 48; Humphrey Llwyd, *Commentarioli Britannicae Descriptionis Fragmentum* (Cologne, 1572), 65ʳ.

[77] Prys, in a marginal note in Llanstephan MS 43, 30, cites 'Andr. Hipperius de succubis et incubis' as his source. The relevant lines (Williams, *Ymryson*, 9.21–34) are based on a section in *Methodi Theologiae* (Basel, 1574), 302–6, 'Vtrum daemones assumant corpora, & an aliqui ex illis fiant incubi & succubi'.

[78] Williams, *Ymryson*, 9.31–6.

[79] *Ibid*. 43.60.

[80] Josephine Waters Bennett, *The Rediscovery of Sir John Mandeville* (New York, 1954), 243.

Other works bracketed with the Travels by Prys on account of their untruths were the tale of Huon of Bordeaux, Aesop's fables, and unspecified works of Ovid:[81] there were other instances of disapproval of all these works in sixteenth-century England.[82] Yet in an age of keen religious sensibilities and moral earnestness, censure of such works was very far from being solely a Protestant phenomenon. Vives had expressly disapproved of both medieval romances and of Ovid, whilst Erasmus too had dismissed the romances, including stories of Arthur and Lancelot, as 'fabulae stultae et aniles'.[83] His Protestant prejudices apart, Prys's attitude towards some of the works he censured partly reflected a common humanist disdain for such materials.

If Prys considered the eulogistic tradition central to Welsh bardism to be suspect because it encouraged mendacity, what did he propose to replace it? Given his priestly calling and theological background, it is not surprising that he was a champion of divine poetry. Having castigated Cynwal for the mendacity of his eulogies, he significantly asserts that the only true poetry was that sung in praise of God.[84] And it is apparent that the divine poetry he favoured was that based on Scripture. In the twenty-fifth poem of the debate, in response to Cynwal's charge that he had no bardic teacher, Prys proudly claims the Bible as his teacher, before proceeding to extol it as the source of the free muse – 'the perfect muse of pure faith' – which had been eloquent in the Church in praising God.[85] Prys was eager to see the Bible become part of the cultural inheritance of Welsh poets: 'The chronicle of every true poet,' he said, 'is the beloved Word of God, let the harpstring be tuned!'[86] It is clear that Prys exulted in the increased contemporary dissemination of the Bible, a central cultural accomplishment of Protestant humanism. This is most apparent in the forty-fourth poem of the debate, where he delights in the blessedness of the age compared to times past because of the new accessibility of the Bible. By virtue of the availability of God's Word, it was a better time for poets to craft their song (*Amser gwell am assio'r gerdd*).[87] Prys's biblical emphasis is interesting given that the debate took place during the years 1581 to 1588, and that in the latter year William Morgan cited him in the preface to his Welsh translation of the Bible as one of those who had given

[81] Williams, *Ymryson*, 42.39–44.

[82] The tale of Huon was among the works censured in the *Summary Declaration of Faith, Uses and Observances in England* (1539), by Thomas Nashe in *The Anatomie of Absurditie* (1589) and by Francis Meres in *Palladis Tamia* (1598); see E. H. Miller, *The Professional Writer in Elizabethan England* (Cambridge, MA, 1959), 79; Vernon Hall, Jr, *Renaissance Literary Criticism* (New York, 1945), 204, 207. Aesop's fables were attacked by the Puritan preacher Edward Dering, a Cambridge contemporary of Prys, in his *Necessary Catechism* (1572); see Louis B. Wright, *Middle-Class Culture in Elizabethan England*, new edn (Ithaca, 1958), 231. Sixteenth-century disapproval of Ovid was common; for examples see Baldwin, *Shakspere's Small Latine and Lesse Greek*, i, 109–13; Frederick S. Boas, *Ovid and the Elizabethans* (London, 1947), 13.

[83] J. W. H. Atkins, *English Literary Criticism: the Renascence*, reprint (New York and London, 1968), 60–1.

[84] Williams, *Ymryson*, 51.33–4.

[85] *Ibid.* 25.137–42.

[86] *Ibid.*47.13–14.

[87] *Ibid.* 44.102.

him assistance.[88] Prys's awareness of the progress of Morgan's translation is probably reflected in the twenty-third poem of the debate, where he foresees not only spiritual benefit but also advantages for the language and its poetry among the consequences of obtaining God's Word 'perfectly in our own language' (*Yn berffaith i'n hiaith yn hvn*).[89]

In an age in which religious sensibilities were well honed, the impulse to produce an explicitly Christian literature – not new, of course, but now pursued with a more sustained earnestness – was manifested in both Catholic and Protestant countries. It lay, for example, at the heart of the desire for a Christian epic: this was the age which produced works such as Vida's *Christiad* and Tasso's *Gerusalemme Liberata*. Protestant poets were disposed to base their divine poetry on the Scriptures, a tendency reflected in the vogue of genres such as the Biblical epic and versifications of the Psalms. In 1574, a few years before the debate, the French Protestant poet Du Bartas, in his highly influential 'L'Uranie' (published in a volume significantly entitled *La Muse Chrestiene*), had urged that poets should sing of Noah rather than Deucalion, of Lazarus's resurrection rather than that of Hippolytus.[90] In his advocacy of a biblically based divine poetry, there is no doubt that Prys was reflecting a literary ideal that had much currency and appeal in contemporary Protestant Europe.

I shall now turn to the second of Prys's main charges against Cynwal. Just as Du Bellay, in 'Le Poète courtisan', had criticized French poets for their lack of learning and Thomas Nashe, in *The Anatomie of Absurditie*, had characterized English popular poets as 'vnlearned sots',[91] so Prys too accuses Cynwal of being deficient in learning. 'I did not find . . . the learning I had expected,' he says of the work of his adversary in the seventeenth poem,[92] a theme later much repeated. This charge, first made in relation to Cynwal's answers to specific questions asked of him about Merlin, Prester John and, somewhat quaintly, the characteristics of the cuckoo, was remorselessly amplified by Prys into a more serious accusation of a general lack of learning.

In essence, Prys's complaint against Cynwal was that his verse lacked substance, *Byr ddeynydd mewn barddoniaeth*, as he put it.[93] He elaborated upon this

---

[88] *Y Beibl Cyssegr-lan* (London, 1588), sig. [*iv], where Prys, David Powell, and Richard Vaughan are cited by Morgan as ones who had given him 'opem . . . non contemnendam' in relation to the work. The extent of these scholars' contribution has been much discussed: it is now generally agreed that their contribution is likely to have been indirect and did not extend to actual translation.

[89] Williams, *Ymryson*, 23.97–104.

[90] For a text of the poem (first published in 1574) see U. T. Holmes, Jr, J. C. Lyons, and R. W. Linker (eds), *The Works of Guillaume De Salluste Sieur Du Bartas* (Chapel Hill, 1938), II, 172–85. For the passage cited see *ibid.* 182–3 (lines 205–8). It was the 1579 edition of *La Muse Chrestiene* which was known in England; see Anne Lake Prescott, *French Poets and the English Renaissance* (New Haven and London, 1978), 271. For an account of the influence of 'L'Uranie' in England see *ibid.* 167–239 *passim*; Lily B. Campbell, *Divine Poetry and Drama in Sixteenth-Century England* (Cambridge, 1959), 74–92.

[91] H. Chamard (ed.), *Joachim Du Bellay: Oeuvres Poétiques* (Paris, 1931), VI, 129–37; R. B. McKerrow (ed.), *The Works of Thomas Nashe*, new edition (Oxford, 1958), I, 24–5.

[92] Williams, *Ymryson*, 17.31–2.

[93] *Ibid.* 23.5.

in a passage in the twenty-second poem of the debate.[94] Conceding Cynwal's metrical mastery, he compared the process of poetic composition to that of housebuilding, urging his adversary to seek timber, stones, and lime to strengthen his edifice. In a trenchant couplet, developing the same metaphor, he summarized his criticism of Cynwal: 'It is foolishness . . . for a fine carpenter to measure the wind' (*Ffoledd, drwy anoff helynt, / I saer gwych fesuro gwynt*).[95] A similar standpoint, that substance should not be subordinate to metrical mastery, is found in the works of other humanist critics. According to Sir Thomas Elyot in *The boke named the Gouernour*, 'they that make verses / expressynge therby none other lernynge but the craft of versifyeng' were not poets but mere rhymesters.[96] An aspect of the critical revolution effected by the Pléiade was a rejection of the notion that skill in complex forms of verse was the test of poetry.[97] The change in the critical climate was reflected in Etienne Pasquier's remark in his *Recherches de la France* that the work of the once admired *grand rhétoriqueur* Guillaume Cretin contained 'prou de rime et équivoques . . . mais peu de raison'.[98] Such statements, like Prys's criticism of Cynwal, constituted a humanist reaction to the medieval tendency to view poetic excellence largely in terms of metrical virtuosity and technical accomplishment.

Prys's emphasis on learning had manifold origins. Among them was a conviction concerning the once erudite nature of Welsh bardism. In the debate he clearly displays his familiarity with the *Scriptorum Illustrium Maioris Brytanniæ . . . Catalogus* of John Bale (1557), an influential but sometimes misleading work where ancient Welsh poets had been depicted as forerunners of Renaissance university men versed in multiple branches of knowledge. (An example was the depiction of the poet Meugant as a philosopher, mathematician, and physician supposedly associated with the *gymnasium* of Chester.[99]) To those like Prys who had swallowed this fictitious version of the Welsh bardic past, contemporary poets such as Cynwal inevitably appeared to be unworthy heirs to a once glorious tradition. It is no wonder that Prys compared Cynwal unfavourably with Taliesin and the two Merlins,[100] poets whom he claimed had been astronomers and natural philosophers.[101] Regret at the passing of the learned tradition of the bards as it had been depicted by Bale's overwrought imagination was certainly one element which fuelled Prys's criticism of Cynwal.

In claiming that Cynwal lacked learning, it is clear that Prys had in mind the kind of humanistic learning with which his own university training had

---

[94] *Ibid.* 22.59–72.

[95] *Ibid.* 22.71–2.

[96] Thomas Elyot, *The boke named the Gouernour* (London, 1531), sig. G1ʳ.

[97] J. E. Spingarn, *Literary Criticism in the Renaissance* (New York and London, 1899), 192.

[98] Quoted by Warner Forrest Patterson, *Three Centuries of French Poetic Theory* (Ann Arbor, 1935), i, 728.

[99] John Bale, *Scriptorum Illustrium Maioris Brytanniæ . . . Catalogus* (1557), 47.

[100] Williams, *Ymryson*, 9.13–18.

[101] *Ibid.* 27.29–38.

endowed him and which he mistakenly thought the ancient Welsh bards also to have possessed. In one poem he specifically bemoaned the fact that Cynwal did not have greater linguistic and scientific knowledge.[102] He sought to elevate such learning above the medieval lore to which Cynwal obstinately clung: there was 'better learning' (*dysg well*), he said, to be found in Mün- ster's *Cosmographia* and the work of Euclid than in Mandeville's Travels so credulously cited by Cynwal.[103] Moreover, he explicitly disparaged the bardic education which Cynwal and his like had received: Cynwal's bardic degree he dismissed as a mere beggar's licence.[104] If bards wanted degrees, it would be better for them to seek the university schools where a higher form of learning could be found; failure to do so, he prophesied, would lead to their demise in a changing cultural world.[105] It is clear that Prys hoped for the emergence of a new type of Welsh poet, one learned in the humanist sense, one who was 'a master of exotic language' and 'a philosopher of wise utter- ance'.[106] Such poets would deploy the new learning as their subject matter as had poets in other countries. In a remarkable passage in the forty-fifth poem, Prys listed the topics Cynwal should study to provide matter for his verse: history, gold, minerals, plants, birds, trees, precious stones, insects, animals, and fish.[107] Poets, said Prys, should sing the praises of the whole created world (*Mawl byd ar hŷd*).[108] It is clear from this that Prys – like another Welsh humanist, Siôn Dafydd Rhys[109] – was eager to see the emergence in Welsh of scientific poetry, then much in vogue in humanist Europe, particularly France and Italy.[110] Only a few years before the debate, in 1578, the most popular of such scientific poems had been published, Du Bartas's encyclo- paedic sacred epic *La Sepmaine*,[111] much celebrated amongst university men in England.[112] (Gabriel Harvey, Prys's Cambridge contemporary, considered Du Bartas, together with Euripides, to be the wisest poet of all time.[113]) In his

---

[102] *Ibid.* 48.45–50.
[103] *Ibid.* 42.55–62, 71–2.
[104] *Ibid.* 23.84.
[105] *Ibid.* 23.85–92.
[106] *Ibid.* 17.94, 27.46.
[107] *Ibid.* 45.35–56.
[108] *Ibid.* 63–6.
[109] In his celebrated 'Letter to the Bards' (1597), Rhys (see note 71) urged Welsh poets to expand their subject matter by having recourse to the works of natural philosophers, mathematicians, astronomers, astrologers, and metaphysicians (*anianolion philosophyddion, mathematicyddion, astronomyddion, astrologyddion a metaphysicyddion*). For a text of the 'Letter' see Thomas Jones (ed.), *Rhyddiaith Gymraeg: Yr Ail Gyfrol* (Cardiff, 1956), 159. The letter is discussed by Branwen Jarvis, 'Llythyr Siôn Dafydd Rhys at y Beirdd', *Llên Cymru*, 12 (1972–3), 45–56.
[110] For an account of French scientific poetry see Albert-Marie Schmidt, *La Poésie scientifique en France au seizième siècle* (Paris, 1938). For an anthology see Dudley Wilson (ed.), *French Renaissance Scientific Poetry* (London, 1974).
[111] For a text of the poem see Holmes, Lyons, and Linker, *Guillaume De Salluste Sieur Du Bartas*, II, 193–440.
[112] Prescott, *French Poets and the English Renaissance*, 198. On the poem's general vogue and influence in England see *ibid.* 167–234, *passim*; H. Ashton, *Du Bartas en Angleterre* (Paris, 1908); A. H. Uppham, *The French Influence in English Literature* (New York, 1911), 145–218, *passim*.
[113] G. C. Moore Smith, *Gabriel Harvey's Marginalia* (Stratford-upon-Avon, 1913), 115.

cornucopian poem Du Bartas had indeed sang the praises of all creation as
Prys urged Welsh poets to do; there is little doubt that the passage to which
I have referred was inspired by *La Sepmaine*, its *troisieme jour, cinquiesme jour,*
and *sixiesme jour* in particular.

When Prys claimed, as he did in the debate's fiftieth poem, that 'A poet
must have learning to compose a proper oration',[114] he was stating a commonplace of Renaissance literary criticism. It was often stated in Italy, as in
Giovanni Pietro Capriano's assertion (1555) that 'Dottrina & cognitione
vniversale & amplissima' were essential poetic requirements.[115] It was similarly
emphasized in France, where Du Bellay asserted that 'ce qui est le com-
mencement de bien ecrire, c'est le scavoir'.[116] He conceived of the poet as
one 'instruict de tous bons ars et sciences, principalement naturelles et math-
ematiques',[117] a requirement amplified by the polymathic Peletier du Mans,
who demanded that 'à notre poëte est necessaire la connaissance d'astrolo-
gie, cosmographie, géométrie, physique, bref de toute la philosophie'.[118]
Such ambitious ideals were expressed in England, too, Gabriel Harvey asserting that 'It is not sufficient for poets to be superficial humanists: but they
must be exquisite artists, & curious vniuersal schollers'.[119] Whilst such declara-
tions reflected the Renaissance's passion for learning, they may also have
reflected classical influences, such as Cicero and Quintilian's prescriptions
concerning the education of the orator.[120] And another influence was
Horace's assertion in his *Ars Poetica*, 'Scribendi recte sapere est et principium
et fons',[121] *sapere* in this context being often understood in Renaissance times
as 'to know' (such an interpretation clearly inspiring Du Bellay's first quoted
remark above).[122] The well established tradition of praising individual
poets for their learning may also be cited in this context, examples being
the plaudits awarded to Homer by Strabo, Quintilian, and the Pseudo-
Plutarchian *De Homeri poesi*, and to Virgil by Servius and Macrobius.[123] Such
critical attitudes persisted into the Renaissance, as in Italian critics' praise
of the erudition of poets such as Dante and Ariosto,[124] and in comments

[114] Williams, *Ymryson*, 50.65–6.
[115] Weinberg, *Literary Criticism in the Italian Renaissance*, 737. For similar prescriptions by other Italian critics
see *ibid.* 97 (A. G. Parrasio), 137, 273 (A. Lionardi), 283 (B. Tasso), 322 (T. Correa), 387 (F. Pedemonte), 722
(B. Daniello), 743 (A. S. Minturno), 749 (J. C. Scaliger). See also Hall, *Renaissance Literary Criticism*, 67.
[116] *Deffence et Illustration de la Langue françoyse*, ed. H. Chamard (Paris, 1904), 179.
[117] *Ibid.* 233.
[118] *L'Art Poëtique*, ed. André Boulanger (Paris, 1930), 216–17 (orthography modified).
[119] Smith, *Harvey's Marginalia*, 161.
[120] *De Oratore* 1.5.17–20; *Institutio Oratoria* 1.10.
[121] Horace, *Ars Poetica* 309.
[122] Clements, *Critical Theory and Practice of the Pléiade*, 47; Du Bellay, *Deffence et Illustration de la Langue
françoyse*, 179n.
[123] For references see O. B. Hardison, Jr, *The Enduring Monument*, new edn (Westport, 1973), 5; Curtius,
European Literature, 206; Weinberg, *Literary Criticism in the Italian Renaissance*, 44, 868, 964; J. W. H. Atkins, *English Literary Criticism: the Medieval Phase* (Cambridge, 1943), 34–5.
[124] Weinberg, *Literary Criticism in the Italian Renaissance*, 283 (B. Tasso), 823 (P. Giambullari), 828 (L.
Benucci), 868 (S. Speroni), 869 (L. Salviati), 869–70 (F. Patrizi), 963–4 (G. B. Pigna), 1045 (G. Malatesta).

such as Harvey's about Chaucer and Lydgate, lauded by him for their 'Astronomie, philosophie, & other parts of profound or cunning art. Wherein few of their time were more exactly learned.'[125]

References in the debate clearly indicate that Prys considered the *doctus poeta* to possess distinct practical advantages over his unlearned comrades. In a letter addressed to Cynwal after receiving his sequence of nine poems, Prys chided him for his dilatoriness in producing his verse, contrasting the professional poet's slowness with his own speed of composition, which he attributed to his book learning: 'and I have only to open books to have plenty of material, the history and nature of everything'.[126] And the learned poet's advantage lay not only in terms of *inventio*. His learning was also vital in providing models for imitation (*imitatio*), a central aspect of Renaissance theories of composition. This was a feature which Prys elaborated upon in a passage originally included in the twenty-fourth poem of the debate,[127] where he cited Horace, Homer, and Ovid and the late medieval Welsh poets Guto'r Glyn and Tudur Aled as 'excellent men, ancient authors' (*Hynod wŷr, hen awdvriaid*) whose work he had studied and to whose example he directly attributed his poetic accomplishments.

Having discussed Prys's contribution to the debate at some length, it is now necessary for us to consider that of his adversary. It must be emphasized at the outset that Cynwal played a decidedly secondary role. Indeed, he was a somewhat reticent debater: 'Old Cato, are you still alive?' asked Prys at the start of the ninth poem, having waited nine months for an answer to his previous poem![128] Compared with Prys, he lacked motivation to fan the flames of debate: responding to Prys's prophecy of woe for the bards unless they came to terms with the new learning, Cynwal's response was 'You will not see the world so'.[129] He felt no need to champion bardic learning as Prys had championed humanism. Faced with the intellectually energetic and aggressive archdeacon, it was Cynwal's complacency which accounted to some extent for his somewhat lacklustre performance.

Cynwal did respond with vigorous denials to Prys's charges of mendacity, which was a matter of personal honour; he stoutly asserted too the existence of a single muse, and that of heavenly origin. He also responded to Prys's challenges to demonstrate his knowledge of specific subjects, such as Merlin, Prester John, and the history of the early colonization of Britain. But those comments of Prys which related to the future direction of Welsh poetry hardly elicited any response from him. In fairness, it must be said that he may not have seen Prys's final sequence of sixteen poems, including the

---

[125] Smith, *Harvey's Marginalia*, 160–1.
[126] Williams, *Ymryson*, C (Prys's letter).5–7.
[127] On the textual status of these lines (omitted from Llanstephan MS 43, but occurring in the β text) see note 37. They are printed with the textual variants in Williams, *Ymryson*, 110.
[128] Williams, *Ymryson*, 9.2.
[129] *Ibid.* 32.41–2.

notable forty-fifth poem specifying the learning which befitted a poet; yet his responses to the poems he did see did not suggest that he would have responded positively to Prys's later poems. For Cynwal's basic standpoint – oft repeated in different words – was that a man such as Prys had nothing to teach him in matters poetic as he was not a professional poet. 'You are a preacher . . . I am a poet,' he said in the eighth poem, 'In divinity and similarly in art I yield the field to you . . . In matters relating to verse grant me precedence accordingly.'[130] In such unreconstructed trade union fashion he insisted on this strict demarcation between priest and poet time and time again, asserting, for example, in the tenth poem that he would be laughed at if he ascended a pulpit to preach, and that Prys was likewise the butt of ridicule for dabbling in matters poetic;[131] elsewhere, pressing the same point, he quotes a Welsh version of the proverb 'Let not the cobbler go beyond his last'.[132] Declaring that the respective callings of Prys and himself as priest and poet had been divinely ordained, he implied that Prys was guilty of flouting the divine order by pretending to be a poet.[133] To this he joined another charge, namely that Prys was guilty of debasing his priestly calling by engaging in poetic combat and indulging in satire, the work of the lowliest dung-hill poet; in this Cynwal echoed the demarcation of poetic functions adopted in the fourteenth-century Welsh bardic grammar.[134] More than once he urged Prys to abandon satire and return to his duties of caring for souls and preaching.[135] Interestingly, Prys had been similarly exhorted in an earlier debate between him and another poet, Siôn Phylip.[136] Both Phylip and Cynwal employed what would have been obvious arguments to a professional poet engaged in debate with an intrusive clerical amateur. Did not the Statute of Gruffudd ap Cynan – the early Tudor document which governed the practice of professional bardism – explicitly prohibit the practice of two arts?[137] And in the circumstances, it was not wholly unexpected that Cynwal should urge his irritatingly persistent adversary to return to preaching.

More than once in the debate Cynwal boasted of his bardic degrees, awarded at the Caerwys eisteddfod of 1567 and later at a nuptial feast.[138] He reproached Prys for lacking such qualifications: his preaching was licensed, but not his poetry.[139] Prys also lacked a regular bardic education under a qualified master

[130] *Ibid.* 8.57–64.
[131] *Ibid.* 10.49–58.
[132] *Ibid.* 14.5–6.
[133] *Ibid.* 8.65–72; 18.11–14.
[134] *Ibid.* 18.23–8. For the bardic grammar's classification of satire as a function of low-grade poets see *Gramadegau'r Penceirddiaid*, ed. G. J. Williams and E. J. Jones (Cardiff, 1934), 56.
[135] In particular, Williams, *Ymryson*, 20.91–102.
[136] John Wyn Roberts, 'Edmwnd Prys: hanes ei fywyd a chasgliad o'i weithiau' (unpublished University of Wales M.A. thesis, 1938), LVII.51–64.
[137] Thomas Parry, 'Statud Gruffudd ap Cynan', *The Bulletin of the Board of Celtic Studies*, V (1929–31), 26.
[138] In particular, Williams, *Ymryson*, 20.47–56.
[139] *Ibid.* 10.61–4.

poet, as Cynwal was to remind him: 'If you are a poet . . . who is your teacher?'[140] A poet who lacked both qualifications and a teacher was automatically suspect: Cynwal attributed both Prys's allegedly faulty *cynghanedd* and his use of only one of the twenty-four metres of classical bardism to his lack of a bardic degree.[141] Cynwal considered Prys – or at least affected to consider him – an interloper, ignorant of both the finer points of bardic technique and of the conventions of bardic life. At the start of the debate, having received Prys's request for his yew bow, Cynwal, in a letter he wrote to accompany his poetic response, reminded Prys that it was customary to trace the recipient's genealogy in a request poem:[142] the amateur Prys did not know bardic protocol. Later in the debate he charged Prys with not knowing that bardic degrees could be awarded at nuptial feasts,[143] and of ignorance of the Statute of Gruffudd ap Cynan. 'It is we poets . . . who know of that,' said Cynwal of the Statute:[144] the phrase 'we poets' (*nyni feirdd*) is, of course, highly indicative. Cynwal displayed in the debate what was in essence a trade guild mentality, casting himself as the jealous guardian of poetic exclusivity.

Prys's response to Cynwal's obscurantist stance is not without interest. Not unexpectedly, he energetically asserted his right to exercise what he termed his 'two offices'.[145] He devoted the fiftieth poem of the debate to this matter, citing a list of clerical predecessors who had also been poets: Petrarch, Thomas à Kempis, Gunther of Pairis, and the Welsh poets Master Harri of Kidwelly, 'Sir' Dafydd Owain, and 'Sir' Owain ap Gwilym.[146] On a broader level, he also countered Cynwal's emphasis on poetic exclusivity by asserting the unity of all the arts – something of a Renaissance commonplace – citing Cicero as his authority:[147] the passage was based on *Pro Archia*, but also contained elements derived from *De Finibus* and *De Oratore*.[148] To the same end, he also cited a favourite Renaissance exemplum illustrative of interdependency, the tale of the belly and the body members (found in both Livy and Plutarch),[149] afterwards proceeding to laud the practice of more than one art and to exult in his own skill in Cynwal's own art of poetry. Cynwal's charge that he lacked a bardic degree and proper bardic instruction was energetically countered by Prys at various points in the debate. Turning defence into attack, he claimed that a supposedly 'unqualified' poet could possess

---

[140] *Ibid.* 18.59–60.
[141] *Ibid.* 12.79–82; 31.43–58.
[142] *Ibid.* prose passage B (summary of Cynwal's letter).4–5.
[143] *Ibid.* 32.23–8.
[144] *Ibid.* 36.19–20.
[145] *Ibid.* 13.58.
[146] *Ibid.* 50.19–30.
[147] *Ibid.* 50.31–42.
[148] *Pro Archia poeta* 1.2. Cf. *De Finibus*, 3.62–3; *De Oratore* 3.20–1.
[149] Williams, *Ymryson*, 50.43–52. Cf. Livy, *Ab Urbe Condita* 2.32.9–11; Plutarch, *Caius Marcius Coriolanus* 6.3–4. On the sixteenth-century popularity of this exemplum see Baldwin, *Shakspere's Small Latine and Lesse Greek*, ii, 321–2.

superior poetic technique, citing various technical faults in Cynwal's poems.[150] Cynwal's emphasis on formal bardic instruction was dismissed with the mischevious claim that a man of learning could acquire the bardic metres in a month or two on his own, achieving a greater mastery than Cynwal possessed.[151] And just as he listed clerics who were also poets, so he produced a list of renowned Welsh amateur poets, all of whom he claimed were better than Cynwal.[152]

It will be seen that Cynwal does not escape lightly: personal disparagement was very much the stuff of Welsh bardic debates. But it must not be thought that Prys was solely concerned with putting down his immediate adversary. His disparagement of Cynwal is likely to have been symptomatic in some measure of his attitude to the general run of contemporary Welsh professional poets.[153] In the poem where he cited renowned amateur poets, he referred too to his famous kinsman, the humanist William Salesbury, translator of the Welsh New Testament and something of a Renaissance polymath. Earlier in the debate Cynwal had praised Salesbury's learning but had noted in passing that he was not a poet.[154] Prys's retort was scathing: Salesbury, he said, should not be compared to what he called 'you poets' (the original Welsh *chwi'r glêr* is more derogatory, as *y glêr* were low-grade poets).[155] He should rather be compared to 'we, masters of art, possessed of many languages and the seven arts'.[156] The contrast is pointed: on the one hand, 'you poets', who knew neither arts nor languages; on the other, cognoscenti such as Salesbury and Prys himself, versed in humanist learning. Prys's declaration of humanist solidarity was interestingly paralleled by Francesco Berni in his *Dialogo contra i Poeti* of 1526. Berni too had disparaged professional poets as a class, affirming the superiority of such as Vida, Pontano, Bembo, and Sannazaro, humanists who wrote poetry but who were so much more than mere poets.[157]

The Prys–Cynwal debate was more than a clash between individual poets. The two protagonists also spoke for two significant cultural factions in sixteenth-century Wales, the university-educated humanists and the professional poets. It would not be amiss to view the debate as a clash between the old and the new, the protagonists representing respectively an essentially medieval mindset and one influenced by the culture of the new learning.[158]

---

[150] Williams, *Ymryson*, 13.31–42; 22.19–32; C (Prys's letter).15–17, 50–5.

[151] *Ibid.* 52.63–8.

[152] *Ibid.* 48.57–72. The poets cited were Dafydd Llwyd of Mathafarn (*c.* 1395–1486), Gruffudd ab Ieuan ap Llywelyn Fychan (*c.* 1485–1553), Huw ap Rhys Wyn (fl. 1550) and Wiliam Midleton (*fl.* 1550–?1596).

[153] Prys's attitude to the professional bards was, in practice, dichotomous; he enjoyed their company, entertaining them at his home in Maentwrog (National Library of Wales MS 11993, 25; Tan-y-bwlch MS, 563).

[154] *Ibid.* 32.51–8.

[155] *Ibid.* 48.35–8.

[156] *Ibid.* 48.41–2.

[157] Spingarn, *Literary Criticism in the Renaissance*, 153–4.

[158] Cf. Thomas Parry, *Hanes Llenyddiaeth Gymraeg hyd 1900* (Cardiff, 1945), 161; Ceri Davies, *Welsh Literature and the Classical Tradition* (Cardiff, 1995), 80–1, and my own remarks in Williams, *Ymryson*, clxxxv.

It is true that there were traditional elements in Prys's thinking: it would be wrong to assume too stark a dichotomy between the Middle Ages and the Renaissance. Yet it cannot be doubted that Prys's cultural persona was moulded by the prevailing standards of contemporary humanistic culture. His dual advocacy of the learned and the divine in poetry reflected a synthesis which was typical of the culture of the Christian humanism of the Renaissance.

The debate took place at a time of crisis for Welsh poetry. Remarkable, in Sidney's words, for 'long continuing', the tradition represented by bards such as Cynwal was artistically arthritic and enfeebled, its energies, such as they were, almost exclusively directed into the well-worn channels of bardic eulogy. Dependent on the patronage of the gentry, a class gradually becoming more Anglicized and increasingly attracted by new cultural fashions emanating from Renaissance England, the long-term prospects for the bards were not auspicious. In this context, Prys's advocacy of new kinds of poetry in opposition to the prevailing tradition of bardic eulogy is of considerable interest. Divine, scripturally based poetry became a practical possibility with the advent of the Welsh Bible. Yet, apart from metrical psalms – a field in which Prys himself was eventually to excel – little poetry of this kind was produced in late Renaissance Wales. The dominance of *cynghanedd* in Welsh poetry undoubtedly played a part in this respect. Prys touched upon this at one point in the debate. He was familiar, he said, with poetry in eight languages; nowhere, however, had he found metrical systems which were as restrictive as those of Welsh. All its metres were strict (i.e. they employed *cynghanedd*), and God's Word transcended poetic metre.[159] Significantly, when he came to write his metrical psalms, Prys abandoned the strict classical metres and employed a popular metre devoid of *cynghanedd*. The dominance of *cynghanedd* undoubtedly militated against the development of the more ambitious genres of divine poetry; as the Italian-based Welsh humanist Gruffydd Robert noted in his grammar, epic poetry was incompatible with the classical metres which employed *cynghanedd*.[160]

Similar metrical considerations also applied in relation to the other type of poetry favoured by Prys, learned scientific poetry. But in this regard there were other difficulties too. The development of such a poetry was contingent upon the emergence of a new type of poet versed in humanist culture, a point implicit in Prys's exhortations that bards should seek university learning. Linguistic considerations were also applicable in this case. Unless Welsh became a medium for learned discourse in the arts and sciences – and for a number of reasons that was unlikely – the Welsh poet who sought to write scientific poetry would have to be something of a linguistic innovator. Such difficulties were not insurmountable; yet they were considerable, and it is not

---

[159] *Ibid.* 17.75–82.
[160] *Gramadeg Cymraeg gan Gruffydd Robert*, ed. Williams, [330]. Robert urged aspiring writers of Welsh epics to adopt 'such metres as the Italians use' (*[y] fath fessurau y mae'r eidalwyr yn i arfer*).

surprising that no one – not even Edmwnd Prys himself – ventured to produce scientific poetry in Welsh.

It is evident, I think, that Prys's literary programme was one in essence best suited to amateur poets such as himself; given the relatively small Welsh reading public, divine and scientific poetry could not have sustained professional bardism as the eulogistic tradition, with its customized products appealing to individual gentry patrons, had done. But, as I have suggested, there were forces at work in late sixteenth-century Wales which would eventually lead to the loss of gentry patronage and the demise of professional bardism. The future belonged to Prys and his ilk rather than to Cynwal. Though Prys's literary ideals were not precisely realized, the debate is important in pointing towards a new age in Welsh poetry, an age less dominated by eulogy, where poets would be exclusively amateurs who composed poetry for their own delectation in accordance with their own tastes and interests. I hope that I have shown that it is also noteworthy in that it preserves a critical voice – that of Edmwnd Prys – which declares common Renaissance values, one which, I believe, deserves to be drawn to the attention of students of Renaissance literature outside Wales.

University of Wales, Aberystwyth

4

Classical voices in Buchanan's hexameter psalm paraphrases

ROGER P. H. GREEN

In a previous paper in this journal[1] I examined five of George Buchanan's psalm paraphrases, in which his versions were presented in the likeness of Horatian odes. In these, Buchanan could be seen not only to recall Horace in metre, language, and style, showing great skill and learning as he did so, but also to engage imaginatively with the classical poet in various ways, without departing from his habitual methods and principles of fairly close paraphrase. The enterprise of paraphrasing psalms in Latin verse, rapidly increasing in popularity in the middle of the sixteenth century, at the time when he wrote, certainly had devotional objectives – it may have begun with the versifying of the Penitential Psalms – and, at least potentially, educational ones, but in Buchanan's hands it was also a verse-form with claims to some literary status, and his versification of the whole Psalter is an important part of his many-sided reputation as a Humanist scholar and neo-Latin poet not only in his native Scotland, but also in France, where he spent much of his early career.[2]

The present paper, also first given in the University of Wales, Swansea – on this occasion in response to the friendly encouragement of Professor Ceri Davies, co-organizer of the conference on Renaissance in the Celtic Lands[3] – concentrates on the paraphrases that he cast in the hexameter metre. The attention of classically oriented readers of the paraphrases is likely to be attracted first by his metrical variety[4] – he uses some thirty metres altogether, without going beyond the classical repertoire – but two-thirds of the psalms are in fact rendered in more familiar metres. The incidence of these is not quite what one might expect: the elegiac metre, ubiquitous and so versatile

---

[1] Roger P. H. Green, 'Davidic psalm and Horatian ode: five poems of George Buchanan', *Renaissance Studies* 14 (2000), 91–111.

[2] For matters biographical (and much else), see the excellent study of I. D. McFarlane, *Buchanan* (London, 1981).

[3] Held at the University of Wales, Swansea, 20 October 2001.

[4] See R. P. H. Green, 'George Buchanan's psalm paraphrases: matters of metre', in I. D. McFarlane (ed.), *Acta Conventus Neo-Latini Sanctandreani, Proceedings of the Fifth International Congress of Neo-Latin Studies* (Binghamton, NY, 1986), 51–60.

in antiquity, is found three times only (88, 114, 137),[5] and the hexameter is used for ten paraphrases in all. The commonest metre is in fact the iambic couplet (i.e. trimeter and dimeter), which occurs twenty-eight times, in almost one fifth of the poems, and there is also the iambic dimeter, used fourteen times. (It is relevant that Buchanan had recently used the iambic metre in his dramas, and technically speaking it is also one of the easier ones, though that is a small consideration except where names and certain words are concerned). Over and above that, there is the combination in sequence of hexameter and iambic trimeter, used no less than sixteen times, and a number of other combinations involving the hexameter. (Composite metres like these, where the hexameter alternates with another metre, are not part of the present study.) The Alcaic and Sapphic metres characteristic of Horace account for twenty-six psalms between them; but – in case any of his admirers are wondering – there are no paraphrases in the hendecasyllablic metre favoured by Catullus. With this exception – presumably Buchanan thought its associations inappropriate for the psalms – the range of metres in the paraphrases broadly reflects the variety within Buchanan's secular poems,[6] at least as far as the mainline ones are concerned.

The bare fact that the hexameter was used ten times may raise few eye-brows, but in fact this was a notable innovation, and even though the first full edition was that of 1565/1566, well after the period in which most of the paraphrases were apparently composed,[7] this would not have been lost on the contemporary reader. The new genre of psalm paraphrase was a highly competitive area[8] – as shown by the remarks of H. Étienne in his introduc-tion to the edition of 1556, in which he used a selection of paraphrases by Buchanan and others to trumpet Buchanan's virtues[9] – and matters of metre were an important aspect of this scholarly rivalry. Leaving aside sporadic paraphrases found among other kinds of composition by various poets or published in works by divers hands, earlier paraphrases are, metrically speak-ing, of three main kinds. There are extensive sets in the elegiac metre by Hessus (1st edn, 1529), Bonade (1531), and Spangeburg (1544); an import-ant series from 1530 on by Macrin[10] and some by Musius, in lyric metres; and a set in the iambic metre by Flaminio, completed by Spinola (1546).[11] In

---

[5] These are studied in J. Wall, 'Buchanan's elegies', in A. J. Aitken, M. P. McDiarmid, and D. S. Thomson (eds), *Bards and Makars* (Glasgow, 1977), 184–93.

[6] There is a useful selection of these in P. Ford, *George Buchanan, Prince of Poets* (Aberdeen, 1982).

[7] According to Buchanan's own *Life* (McFarlane, *Buchanan*, 151 and 247), they were written 'chiefly' (*maxime*) during the time of his imprisonment by the Spanish Inquisition, in 1551–2 (McFarlane, *Buchanan*, 131–51). The date of 1547 given for their inception in my earlier paper (Green, 'Davidic psalm', 92) was a slip, though not impossible.

[8] J. A. Gärtner, 'Latin verse translations of the psalms', *Harvard Theological Review* 49 (1956), 271–305, based on the pioneering work of J. Vaganay and, more securely, the British Library Catalogue.

[9] McFarlane, *Buchanan*, 250.

[10] See Green, 'Davidic psalm', 92 and note 4.

[11] For further details, see Gärtner (note 8) and McFarlane, *Buchanan*, 248.

a class of its own is the ambitious and rather eccentric version of Gagnay (1547), who paraphrased half of the psalms in a remarkable variety of metres, many of them unattempted and unheard of before;[12] they include one in the hexameter metre, to which Buchanan pays the compliment of fleeting imitation.[13]

But Buchanan was not simply interested in metre, or even the questions of elegance, correctness, and fidelity to the original meaning that Gagnay identified in his preface. As with the odes of Horace, engagement with the subject-matter of his models is for him an important part of his task. In the Renaissance, as in antiquity, the hexameter was known as the 'metrum heroicum' or 'heroum', the metre of heroes: it is above all the metre of epic, and although it is also the standard metre for didactic poetry, pastoral and satire, and certain other kinds of writing, it never lost the prestige of this association. One memorable description of the subject-matter of epic was made by Virgil himself, when as a young man – and long before thoughts of an *Aeneid* – he described how he dropped his plan to write of 'kings and battles' after an admonitory tweak of the ear by Apollo.[14] This was one kind of epic matter, but as well as major conflicts – such as those in Homer's *Iliad*, Virgil, and Lucan – it encompassed endurance and adventure – as in Homer's *Odyssey* – and sometimes a quest of some kind – so Apollonius of Rhodes and Valerius Flaccus on the expedition of the Argonauts, as well as in the *Aeneid*. There is generally, as Servius remarked at the beginning of his commentary on the *Aeneid*, a mixture of gods and men and – less conveniently, in the present context – fact and fiction. The action is set in the past – not necessarily the distant past – but there may be explicit reference to the present, notably in the *Aeneid*, where Virgil mixes past with present by the use of prophecy. Characteristic set pieces include the storm, the Funeral Games, and the descent to the underworld.

Buchanan's reason or reasons for choosing the hexameter will be a question of major interest in the discussion of each of the paraphrases examined in this paper. For practical reasons, it would be necessary, even for the perfectionist that Buchanan was,[15] to make a decision quite quickly and not go back on it: trial and error would be time-consuming, and there is virtually no trace of it.[16] Unlike some writers, he restricted himself to one version of each psalm. No doubt he developed an intuition for a suitable metre, like a sculptor selecting a block of stone for his next commission, but it is often not difficult to trace his reasons. Certain psalms, or at least certain passages within them – for of course the typical psalm will have a different approach

---

[12] McFarlane, *Buchanan*, 249, 279–81.

[13] Psalm 2, from which Buchanan takes the parenthetic 'aiunt' ('they say') into his line 5.

[14] Virgil, *Eclogues* 6.3. The motif goes back to Callimachus.

[15] See R. P. H. Green, 'The text of George Buchanan's psalm paraphrases', *The Bibliotheck*, 13 (1986), 3–29, for evidence of Buchanan's continual tinkering with his text.

[16] See on Psalm 85 below, 1.

to matters of genre and unity from classical works – focus on traditional epic areas such as wandering or warfare. Occasionally, but rarely, the metrical properties of a key word will leave no choice; but in fact, many words can serve in more than one metre, and as for Hebrew names, they had always been treated with flexibility as far as prosody was concerned. An important consideration was variety: so the choice of the hexameter for Psalm 1 ruled out its use for others in the vicinity, notably Psalms 2 and 4, though on thematic grounds it would be quite suitable for them, and with Psalm 45 destined for the hexameter, the reasonable claims of Psalm 44 could not be allowed. Buchanan also avoided using the same metre as a predecessor.[17]

This paper will also examine the particular ways in which he exploits the stylistic and thematic repertoire of the epic and other genres associated with the hexameter. What particular features – verbal, grammatical, rhetorical – does he employ in recalling classical writers, and how far, and in what circumstances, does he recall them? It should be borne in mind that Buchanan is a relatively close paraphraser, and as a rule does not go off at a tangent and develop his own thoughts, but sticks closely, verse by verse, to the sense of his original where it is not obscure. This reduces the scope for extensive imitation; but since the genres of Roman antiquity can be said to have had their own styles – though the issue is complicated by overlap and imitation – and since one can readily spot divergences from Buchanan's normal idiom, which is a little lacking in variety, perhaps, though not short of poetic qualities, it is not too difficult to detect his sudden intrusions into another style. As in the case of Horace, some of the markers will be relatively subtle, though we need not doubt their effectiveness for educated readers of the time.

It must also be asked which authors, and what contexts within them, are favoured by Buchanan, and how important, indeed, the original contexts are to him. It is not difficult to draw up a list of authors that he used, making use of familiar criteria, including the appearance of unusual words, or of phrases that combine words in the same striking ways, or of similar phrases set in similar metrical positions, and other features for which direct imitation is the most reasonable explanation; though at the margins of his reading, where a claim depends perhaps on one or two such parallels, the possible influence of an intermediary must be allowed for even if it cannot be demonstrated. One must also beware of saying that Buchanan 'read' or 'knew' such-and-such an author when the evidence is minimal. It is less easy, at least in some cases, to make confident claims about the relevance of the original context to any passages of Buchanan; here it is likely that interpretations will vary, for various reasons. But an informed and cautious judgement of

---

[17] Green, 'Matters of metre', 54.

probability is not an unreasonable guide; in what depth is Buchanan likely to have known his supposed models? How many scholars, even in an age less reliant on the printed page than ours, would remember even a small fraction of the two hundred and fifty stories in Ovid's *Metamorphoses*, or the vicissitudes of Caesar and Pompey, Eteocles and Polynices, and their armies, as well as they did the plot of the *Aeneid*?

A fairly clear and consistent picture of his reading and allusion will emerge, but it must be stressed that the picture of what authors he read and what passages he used is not claimed to be complete. Nor is it intended as a definitive contribution to the question of what books Buchanan owned or read – not always the same thing – for which a much broader set of evidence is required.[18] The present work is not a catalogue in sheep's clothing, but a study of allusion, and its modes and significances. It is assumed, as will now be clear, that the relationships created with previous texts, and the effects achieved by them, are intentional, and so there is no need for the assumptions, or the language, of intertextuality in the strict sense. The allusions are applied thoughtfully to their new contexts; they are not 'tags' or 'flosculi', simple adornments or mere aids. Although the discipline of verse composition, for those whose curricula or pastimes have included it, is helpful in giving an idea of what Buchanan could or could not do, and how he could have proceeded, experience in this area is misleading if it suggests that classical verse was seen as a quarry, a collection of helpful phrases more or less ready made. Latin texts in our author are not breeze blocks or veneer, nor indeed in this context should they be seen as jewels whose only function is to dazzle.[19]

The hexameter poems to be examined are 1, 18, 45, 78, 85, 89, 104, 107, 132, and 135.[20] They will be taken in this order, with the exception of the first, which (for good cause shown) will be last. Extracts are given where appropriate, and within them I have emphasized certain details in bold to clarify the brief analyses which follow. Spelling and punctuation are normalized, in a way that would not necessarily be appropriate to a critical edition of Buchanan but may help the reader familiar with modern editions of the classics. Sometimes the Vulgate version of part of a psalm – Buchanan surely knew this well, even if he used one or more other versions[21] – will be quoted, to give an impression of his creativity in general or in particular; this will also illustrate his general technique of paraphrasing, though it is not the purpose of this study to comment on that.

---

[18] A valuable contribution is made by McFarlane, *Buchanan*, 527–31.

[19] As argued for the Latin poetry of late antiquity by M. Roberts, *The Jeweled Style in Late Antiquity* (Ithaca and London, 1989).

[20] Buchanan's numbering follows the Hebrew; in most cases subtract one for the Vulgate reference.

[21] The evidence is gradually increasing that he made use of the version printed at Zurich in 1543 by C. Froschoverus; but it could have been one of many.

PSALM 18

Like many of the psalms, Psalm 18 is a personal poem, and for these Buchanan often uses a lighter metre; but its long description of the Psalmist's
rescue by a wrathful God in full panoply, and riding upon the clouds in a
storm, made the choice of metre unproblematic and provides an opportunity
for sustained epic writing that Buchanan seizes with gusto in lines 15–45. As
already stated, the storm is a set piece of epic; there are storms, for example,
in the first books of the *Aeneid* (1.81–141) of Statius' *Thebaid* (1.336–75), and
at the beginning of Odysseus' adventures in the *Odyssey* (5.291–450). Anger,
too, is a conspicuous topic: Achilles in the *Iliad*, Juno (and perhaps Aeneas)
in the *Aeneid*, Caesar in Lucan's *Civil War*. There is no equally sustained
parallel in classical Latin epic to the presentation of a god's righteous anger
manifested in a great storm that we have here, although the notion, and the
motif of the divine thunderbolt, is by no means unfamiliar, as one can see
from Virgil, *Georgics* 1.328–34, *A.* 6.586–94 (the counterfeit thunder of
Salmoneus), and Horace, *Odes* 1.34). Buchanan's passage is accordingly one
derived from many sources. There is no better example of Buchanan's range
of models, and the energy that his writing derives from them; and to give an
idea of how he works up to this level, the paraphrase will be quoted from the
beginning. The words or phrases given in bold indicate the most conspicuous examples of his exploitation of epic vocabulary (though none of his
words would be out of place in a classical epic); many of these details will be
explained in the comments that follow.

> Te, deus alme, canam, te toto pectore amabo
> sancte parens, mea vis, mea sola potentia, turris,
> praesidium, spes et **rebus solamen in arctis**.
> tu clipeus, tu tela mihi, tu certa salutis
> ancora, tu statio tuti pulcherrima portus.   5
> nam simul atque tuas in laudes ora resolvo,
> te venerans, pacemque petens, inimica facessunt
> arma; salus, placidisque comes pax advolat alis.
> Iam me **letiferis mors circumvolverat atra**
> cassibus, obsessum iam me torrentibus **orcus**   10
> impediebat aquis; **Stygia** iam compede vinctus
> haerebam, laqueoque pedem retinente trahebar.
> hic ego deprensus, supplexque humilisque **vocavi**
> **voce** deum, et dubiis clamavi ad sidera rebus.
> Ille super solio **residens** flammantis **olympi**   15
> **audiit** orantem, postquam pervenit in altum
> clamor, et attentas advertit questibus aures;
> protinus e vultu Domini **conterrita tellus**
> **intremuit**, montesque cava **compage soluta**

nutarunt, penitusque imis fremuere cavernis.   20
fumeus afflatu de naribus aestus anhelo
undabat; **rapidae** contorto vertice flammae
ore fluunt, vivaque animant attacta favilla.
utque suum dominum terrae demittat in orbem,
leniter inclinat iussum fastigia caelum;   25
succedunt pedibus fuscae caliginis umbrae.
ille vehens **curru volucri**, cui flammeus ales
lora tenens levibus ventorum adremigat alis;
se circum furvo **nebularum involvit amictu**,
praetenditque cavis piceas in nubibus undas.   30
acribus ex oculis vibratae spicula flammae
discutiunt tristes claro fulgore tenebras.
inde ruit crepitans lapidosae grandinis imber,
discursantque vagae **sinuosa volumina** flammae.
at vero ut sancto **sermone silentia rupit**,   35
protinus **horrifico** tonitru **caelum omne remugit**,
grandinis et crebra tellus crepitante procella
pulsa sonat, ruptisque micant e nubibus ignes;
flammiferaeque volant **magnum per inane** sagittae,
fulguraque **ingeminant**; laticum concussa lacunas   40
pandit hians tellus, et fontibus ora relaxat,
succutiturque pavens, et fundamenta revelat,
et reserat **chaos**. aeterni sic vox tonat oris,
sic formidandae grave spiritus **infremit** irae.

[I shall worship you, kind God; I shall love you with all my heart, holy parent; my strength, my only power, my tower, safeguard, hope and consolation in adversity. You are my shield, my weapons, you are the certain anchor of my salvation, you are the most peaceful site of my safe harbour. For as soon as I open my mouth in your praise, worshipping you and seeking peace, hostile weapons depart; salvation, and its companion, Peace, fly to me with gentle wings (8).

Already black death had wrapped around me with fatal snares, already Hell was holding me fast in its torrential waters, already I was sticking, overcome by the fetters of the underworld, and I was being dragged along with a noose holding my foot. Trapped, at this point I invoked God with my voice, a humble suppliant, and I called to the stars in my critical situation (14).

He, sitting on the throne of burning Olympus, heard my prayer after my shout had arrived on high, and he turned attentive ears to my complaints. Immediately the earth, terrified, trembled from the face of the Lord, and the mountains tottered, with their hollow structure loosened, and roared far down in the deepest caverns (20).

There surged from his nostrils a smoking heat with panting breath; searing flames flow from his mouth as his head turns, and they kindle what they touch with live ash. And so that it may send its Lord down to the earth, the sky, as commanded, gently bends down its lofty heights; black shadows of darkness follow after his feet (27).

Riding upon a flying chariot, on which a flaming winged creature holding the reins steers upon the light wings of the winds, he covers himself around with a dark garment of clouds, and threatens black waters from the hollow clouds. From them there issues a rumbling deluge of stony hail, and billowing folds of wandering flame are suddenly everywhere (35).

But when he broke the silence with his holy speech, immediately the whole heaven bellowed with terrifying thunder, and the earth, struck with storm after resounding storm of hail, resounds, and fires flash from the shattered clouds; and flame-bearing arrows fly through the great void, and the lightnings are redoubled; the smitten earth, gaping, reveals pools of water, and unlooses its surface with springs, and is tossed up as it quakes, and opens up its foundations, and discloses chaos (42).

Thus does the voice of the eternal mouth thunder, so mightily does the breath of his fearful anger reverberate.]

The Vulgate, omitting verse 1, which describes the nature of the psalm:

2. diligam te domine, fortitudo mea.
3. Dominus firmamentum meum, et refugium meum, et liberator meus. Deus meus adiutor meus, et sperabo in eum. Protector meus, et cornu salutis meae, et susceptor meus.
4. Laudans invocabo Dominum, et ab inimicis meis salvus ero.
5. Circumdederunt me dolores mortis, et torrentes iniquitatis conturbaverunt me.
6. Dolores inferni circumdederunt me, praeoccupaverunt me laquei mortis.
7. In tribulatione mea invocavi Dominum, et ad Deum meum clamavi; et exaudivit de templo sancto vocem meam; et clamor meus in conspectu eius introivit in aures eius.
8. Commota est, et contremuit terra; fundamenta montium conturbata sunt et commota sunt, quoniam iratus est eis.
9. Ascendit fumus in ira eius, et ignis a facie eius exarsit; carbones succensi sunt ab eo.
10. Inclinavit caelos, et descendit; et caligo sub pedibus eius.
11. Et ascendit super cherubim, et volavit; volavit super pennas ventorum.
12. Et posuit tenebras latibulum suum; in circuitu eius tabernaculum eius, tenebrosa aqua in nubibus aeris.

13. Prae fulgore in conspectu eius nubes transierunt, grando et carbones ignis.
14. Et intonuit de caelo Dominus, et Altissimus dedit vocem suam, grando et carbones ignis.
15. Et misit sagittas suas, et dissipavit eos; fulgura multiplicavit, et conturbavit eos.
16. Et apparuerunt fontes aquarum, et revelata sunt fundamenta orbis terrarum, ab increpatione tua, Domine, ab inspiratione spiritus irae tuae.

Buchanan begins simply, like the Psalmist, but quickly moves to a more heightened style. In his third line he has inserted a precise allusion to Statius (*Thebaid* 10.590), and the images in the next two lines (his own invention) are from war and seafaring. The tone rises further in lines 9–12, with repeated 'iam' articulating a carefully constructed tricolon. The literal picture in these lines is evidently one of being caught in mud and being trapped in it by a shackled foot; this nightmarish scenario is suggested by the notorious mud and ooze of the Virgilian underworld (*A.* 6.296, 323, 414) recalled in 'Stygia' and 'Orcus', but it also functions effectively at the allegorical level as a picture of spiritual danger.[22]

God hears his cry from on high; the use of epic Olympus is frequent enough in neo-Latin verse to need no special comment. The world is terrified, and the heavens let down their creator; the ensuing storm leaves the earth agape. This magnificent scene is carefully structured by Buchanan, alternating description with movement, developing that movement with unobtrusive particles, and creating a climax with the most unusual but appropriate 'at vero' in line 35 (*A.* 4.279: Aeneas' horror at Mercury's divine message). As in the Vulgate, verbs are very prominent, often at the beginning of the line, as in 'audiit' or 'intremuit'; the first of these is an obsolete by-form of 'audivit' valued by poets for its dactylic impetus in this position. Prominent too are compound adjectives like 'letiferis', 'horrifico', 'flammifer' ('death-bringing', 'fear-making', 'flame-bearing'), formations of a kind common and prolific in the epic style. Nouns and adjectives denoting fire or darkness pack his verse: even Olympus, a snow-covered mountain to the writers of antiquity, is fiery or blazing.

Numerous authors are used, including Virgil, Ovid, Lucan, and Statius. Sometimes the context is important, sometimes it clearly is not: the flame of line 22 recalls the searing or ravaging (not 'rapid') fire of the thunderbolt alluded to in Virgil *A.* 1.42, but the 'sinuosa volumina' of 34 were used of a snake (*A.* 11.753). In line 35, where the angry Jahweh speaks, the second half-line derives from Ovid *M.* 1.208, describing a punitive Jupiter; Buchanan interestingly adds 'sancto' ('holy'). Did he feel a need to detoxify the Ovidian Jupiter, in most of that book a flagrant Don Juan? Lucan supplies 'compage

---

[22] In the Vulgate Buchanan would have found 'dolores mortis' at this point; the 1543 edition has 'funes' (see note 21).

soluta' (19) and 'chaos' (43) from a single, well-known passage about the
end of time and the Stoic conflagration (1.72–4), and 'residens' from a
description of Jupiter (1.198) The phrase emphasized in line 29 is formed
from phrases of Statius (*Thebaid* 1.631 and 3.416) with similar contexts.
Other authors used are Lucretius, who several times has 'magnum per inane'
(cf. line 39), and Horace, who is slightly adapted for 'curru volucri' in line
27 (*Odes* 1.34.8) and for 'mors circumvolverat atra' in line 9 (*Satires* 2.1.58 –
a 'heroic line' according to one commentator).

In the rest of the poem, which is 126 lines long, there are just the occasional
touches of epic, as Buchanan reverts to his normal style and idiom, one which
is by no means prosaic or lifeless, and from which he can readily switch to the
level of epic. The following passage (lines 70 and 71) illustrates this flexibility well:

> te duce perrumpo **florentes aere phalanges**,
> altaque **turrigeri** supero fastigia muri.

[With you as my leader I break through phalanxes flourishing with
bronze, and I overcome (leap over) the high tops of a towered wall.]

Compare, for the first line, Virgil's 'florentis aere catervas' (*A.* 7.804, 11.433);
but why does Buchanan not use 'catervas' (roughly, 'platoons')? His 'phalanges'
– which classical epic does not use in its technical sense of phalanxes – is
considered more effective, having been used twice of the Greeks in the
Aeneid to recall their terrifying army. Likewise, in adding towers to the wall
for the narrator to jump over, he is thinking of a fortified city, whether in
general (*A.* 10.253) or in particular (*A.* 7.631). There are also important
overtones, as will be seen in other contexts, to the sentence 'populos frenare
superbos / imperio facis' ('you make me rein in proud peoples with authority') in lines 109–10; here the Vulgate has 'constitues me in caput gentium'
('you will set me up at the head of the peoples': verse 44).

PSALM 45

This psalm is described in contemporary Latin translations and commentaries as a marriage song ('carmen nuptiale'), or as some kind of love song. In
classical terms, it is an epithalamium, but Buchanan does not recall any of
the classical examples, such as the hexameter epithalamia of Catullus (poem
64) or Claudian (poem 10 Hall), preferring to create a poem which by dint
of scattered but emphatic allusions is strongly Virgilian in texture. As usual,
he avoids a Christological interpretation (this psalm was generally understood of Christ and the Church),[23] and relates it solely to King Solomon;

---

[23] In 89.109 he refers to 'tui Christi', following the Bible translations closely (verse 52), but this does not
refer to Christ; earlier in that poem he translates 'christus' (verse 39) as 'electum regem' (78).

there is a reference to Solomon's Egyptian wife in line 46 ('Pharii proles . . . tyranni'), which Buchanan imports from 1 Kings 9.16 and 2 Chron. 8.11.[24] He is clearly described as 'rex' in lines 4 and 5, following the biblical text, and later in 49 and 60; and his exalted status in line 5 is emphasized with the words 'hominum cui nemo e semine cretus' ('to whom no-one born of the seed of man . . .'), using the rare and poetic word 'cretus'.[25] In line 10 he is described as 'invicte heros' ('invincible hero': for 'invicte', Virgil *A.* 6.365; Aeneas is frequently 'heros'). He is a mounted warrior (a detail not in the Vulgate, but clearly implied in 'inequita' ['ride'] in verse 4 of the 1543 translation), with truth and equity guiding his chariot, and he shoots what are literally 'wound-making' arrows ('vulnificis': cf. Virgil *A.* 8.446 and later epicists). He is beloved by the 'regnator Olympi' ('the ruler of heaven'): interestingly, though perhaps this should not be pressed, this precise description of Jupiter is found on both the occasions when it occurs in Virgil's *Aeneid* in the context of married love, albeit unhappy, at 2.779, where Creusa is making her last farewell, and at 7.558, where Juno is aghast at the thought of Aeneas marrying Lavinia and seeks to prevent it.

The description of Solomon's power that follows is based on two famous passages from the *Aeneid.* In lines 19 and 20 the words 'nec maris aut terrae spatium, nec terminus aevi finiet imperium' ('neither the great size of sea and land, nor the end of time will end this power') amplify the original's 'in saeculum saeculi' ('for ever') by recasting Virgil's 'his ego nec metas rerum nec tempora pono: imperium sine fine dedi' ('for them I set neither boundaries to their authority, nor time-limits: I have given power without end') (*A.* 1.278–9: alluded to again in Psalm 132.30). In line 58 there is a verbally exact echo of 'regere imperio' ('to govern with power') from the exhortation put into the mouth of Anchises in the underworld at *A.* 6.851: 'tu regere imperio populos, Romane, memento' ('you, Roman, remember to govern the peoples with power'). Buchanan's next line uses the word 'populos', combined at the end of the same line with the words 'frenare superbos' ('to rein back the proud'), which echo those of Aeneas in *A.* 1.523 (he is addressing Dido) '(gentis) frenare superbas' ('to rein back proud races': cf. 18.109).[26] Solomon's power will be eternal, like that of the Romans. Returning to the present, his regal handmaidens ('filiae regum' in the Vulgate, at verse 28) are graced with the syntactically distinctive Virgilian phrase 'genus alto a sanguine' ('a family from exalted blood').

The Egyptian queen is introduced in line 30, with the words 'At regina' ('but the queen'), words which though straightforward enough happen to

---

[24] The reference to Ophir in line 32 is also imported by Buchanan; cf. 1 Kings 9.28 and 2 Chron. 8.18 and 9.10.

[25] An archaism used by Virgil and later epicists; the closest parallel to Buchanan's phrase is in fact Ovid *M.* 15.760 'mortali semine cretus', referring to Augustus.

[26] The version printed by Vautrollier in 1580 gives a rather different version of these lines, omitting 'imperio', but the authenticity of the variants in this version cannot be established: see Green, 'The text', pp. 22–3.

be the first words of the fourth book of the *Aeneid*. This may be no accident;
book 4 is the main source for descriptions of her luxurious appearance.
First, the repeated 'auro' ('with gold') in line 31, which adorns her hair and
breasts. One may compare for the repetition the description of Dido in 4.138
and 139 – before the fateful hunt; it is in this array that she and Aeneas will
meet in the cave.[27] Although Buchanan has nothing corresponding to the
fringe of her garment mentioned in his original, this passage could have
commended itself to him as he sought a way of translating the Bible's 'fim-
bria' ('fringe'), a word never found in classical Latin in the metrically helpful
singular form; he might have considered using the word 'limbus' for this
from *A.* 4.137 (where it is qualified by 'picto', which does occur here). More
luxury, and more elaboration from this book of Virgil, surrounds the queen
of Tyre (who is not the bride), 'regina Tyrus'[28] of line 42: note 4.134
'ostroque insignis et auro' – which is echoed in line 47 of the paraphrase, in
'gemmisque insignis et auro' – and 4.262 'Tyrioque ardebat murice'.[29] But
perhaps the most striking allusion here is one from a quite different context,
that in line 50 'dives opum, dives pictai vestis et auri' ('rich in wealth, rich
in embroidered garments and gold': he has now returned to the bride). This
line, conspicuous for its repetition of 'dives' and the choice archaism of
'pictai', is almost identical to *A.* 9.26 ('opum' replaces 'equum' ['in horses']),
a line which has no reference whatever to Dido but describes the appearance
of the mounted Italian army that confronts Aeneas.

Such a line could be taken as encouraging a sceptical construction of the
nature of Buchanan's allusion: surely he is taking suitable words and phrases
from wherever he finds them? Yet there is one more reference to the African
queen. Among other exhortations delivered to the bride is the exhortation
to admire and respect her new husband, 'who hangs from your lips' – that
is, 'dotes on every word you speak': this manner of speaking is actually
extremely rare in Latin – 'tuo qui pendet ab ore', for which compare *A.* 4.79
(Dido) 'pendetque iterum narrantis ab ore'. In an intriguing inversion the
description of the excited Dido is transferred to the bridegroom, who, unlike
Aeneas, is not restricted to the most tenuous expressions of love but, on the
contrary, exhorted to display it. His devotion is further emphasized in the
next line, where he is described as 'pulchris defixus vultibus haeret' ('he
concentrates intently on her beautiful face'); this is influenced by *A.* 1.495
'obtutuque haeret defixus in uno', describing how the pensive Aeneas,
immediately before he meets Dido, reacts to the pictures of the Trojan War
in the vestibule. Neither of these descriptions is required by his model:
Buchanan chose to add them. In this poem it is difficult to escape from

[27] There is a similar use of the word 'auro' by Virgil at *A.* 7.279–80.
[28] This is surely intended to mean 'of Tyre', with 'Tyrus' the genitive singular form of 'Tyro'; but this would
give the name of a heroine, not the city, which is usually 'Tyrus' (genitive 'Tyri').
[29] There is a similarly phrased reference – positively the final reference to Dido – to garments stiff with
gold and purple in *Aeneid* 11.72.

Carthage, and here there is at least the suspicion that the scholar-poet is playing with the notion of a marriage between an Aeneas-figure and a Dido-figure, a union more successful than the one famed in mythology.

In the last four lines the epic tone is maintained with a somewhat more varied palette. Line 60 'nec tu carminibus, regina, tacebere nostris' ('nor will you, queen, be passed over in my songs')[30] combines Virgil's 'nec tu carminibus nostris indictus abibis' ('nor will you depart unsung from my poem': *A.* 7.733) with an echo of 'nec tu . . . silebere' from Ausonius, 24.107;[31] the phrase 'tellus liquido circumsona ponto' ('the land struck by the resounding of the liquid ocean') uses epithets from post-Virgilian epicists; and the expression of eternity 'dumque aurea volvet astra polus' ('and as long as the heavenly axis turns the golden stars') is Buchanan's variation on a common theme, of a kind that will receive further comment in the context of Psalm 89. The source of 'semper celebrabere' in the last line is Virgil *A.* 8.76, from Aeneas' prayer to the Tiber.

PSALM 78

In this, the longest of the psalms for which Buchanan uses the hexameter metre, the main theme is the experiences of the Hebrews in the desert, among them the ordeals of wandering, warfare, suffering, and disobedience. It is the first place in these hexameter poems where Buchanan explicitly gives to the Psalmist the classical – in particular, the Augustan[32] – persona of the 'vates', the inspired poet who pronounces on great matters and from whom the present and future generations ('minores' in line 8)[33] will learn. Using this persona, solemn and formal though not exclusively epic, Buchanan is able to stress that his narratives will have a strongly moral purpose; while in the repeated contrast between what is 'marvellous' and what is 'true' in this opening passage there may be an implicit distancing of the Psalmist from the fictions of epic. The paraphrase begins 'Audite Isacidae' ('hear, descendants of Isaac'), using for the Hebrews[34] a name perhaps of Buchanan's own devising and modelled on the epic-style patronymic – so Virgil's 'Dardanidae' are 'the descendants of Dardanus', i.e. Trojans. It continues with a recollection, in 'huc animos advertite vestros' in the next line, of the

---

[30] Vautrollier (see note 26) prints 'Rex magne' rather than 'regina' here; this alternative passage need not represent an authorial correction, and in this line, although the formula 'nec tu . . .' naturally signals that the spotlight now turns from the queenly bride to another, such an interpretation is not unavoidable.

[31] This and other references to Ausonius follow the numbering in R. P. H. Green (ed.), *Ausonii Opera* (Oxford, 1999).

[32] J. K. Newman, *Augustus and the New Poetry* (Brussels, 1967), ch. 4. The persona is adopted by Virgil in his *Eclogues* and then in his second preface to the *Aeneid* (7.41), and by Horace in various places, including *Epodes* 16.66. See also Green, 'Davidic psalm', 99.

[33] For 'minores' cf. Virgil, *A.* 8.268, where after describing how his followers were saved by Hercules Evander speaks of the maintenance of his worship by 'minores'.

[34] It recurs in line 10 and 'Abramidae' is found in line 114, and both are found in other poems too.

Virgilian phrase 'quae dicam animis advertite vestris' ('mark what I will say
in your minds', *A*. 2.712). Both underpin the vatic stance.

In examining the body of this paraphrase it is not possible to isolate a particularly elaborate passage, as in that of Psalm 18, nor to specify a particularly
resonant emphasis or cluster of emphases, as in that of Psalm 45. What invites
attention is, rather, the consistency of tone which, matching the subject matter,
locates the poem in the epic range and guarantees a pervasive epic voice; a
voice realized partly by allusion to specific passages – though in these cases
the original contexts often do not appear to be germane – and partly by more
generalized uses of the appropriate stylistic repertoire. The following extract
(lines 20–33) shows how he can maintain an epic standard of writing without
the support of specific allusions, but relying on his wide command of language
and idiom and a notable feeling for the dynamics of the classical hexameter.

> Cur suboles Ephraemi, docta sagittis   20
> figere vel iaculo quamvis distantia certo,
> terga dedit paene ante tubas, latebrisque salutem
> (O pudor!) abiectis quaesivit turpiter armis?
> nempe quod aversos flexere per avia gressus,
> obliti legum et monitorum, et foederis icti,   25
> obliti tantorum operum, quae testibus olim
> patribus in Phariis Dominus patraverat oris,
> cum mare divisit sese cumulante profundo
> inter et aggestos undae stagnantis acervos
> incolumem eduxit populum, duce nube, serena   30
> luce, per obscuras flamma praeeunte tenebras.
> flumina de solidi patefecit vulnere saxi,
> damnatisque siti rivos donavit harenis.

[Why did the offspring of Ephraem, taught unerringly to transfix targets
with arrows or spear however far away, turn tail almost before the trumpets
sounded? Why did they seek salvation in darkness, disgracefully throwing
away their arms (for shame!)? Because they directed their wayward footsteps through pathless areas, forgetting the (divine) laws and warnings,
and the established covenant, forgetting those great works which the Lord
had performed in the regions of Egypt, as witnessed by the fathers of old,
when the sea divided itself, with the deep piling itself up, and led out his
people unharmed, with a cloud leading them, among the gathered heaps
of standing water with flame preceding them through the thick darkness.
He opened rivers with a blow to the solid rock, and bestowed streams of
water upon sand condemned to thirst.]

This begins with strong, sarcastic expostulation and an embedded exclama-
tion, and quickly turns to answer his own impassioned questions – the figure

that ancient rhetoricians called 'ratiocinatio' – in a way that his original does not, with 'nempe' . . . (of which 'namely' would be a prosaic translation). In the long and powerful sentence that gives the answer, the redoubled 'obliti' ('forgetful of') in lines 25 and 26 emphasizes the important point, balancing in its twofold answer the similar grammatical forms 'legum' and 'operum', and the elided 'monitorum' and 'tantorum'. In 26–7 'testibus (olim) patribus' is one several examples of the deft use of the ablative absolute which often adds concision and pace to his writing. The description of the crossing of the Red Sea is finely conceived and realized: the deep piles itself up into heaps of standing water – the verb 'stagno' connotes not so much 'stagnant' as 'standing' water. Then the rock is 'wounded' like an enemy, to reveal rivers, and sands condemned to dryness are 'presented' (literally) with watercourses, with the two contrasting verbs mirroring the nature and activity of God.

In the main body of the poem allusions to passages from Virgil and others do occur, but it is often debatable whether there is contextual significance. It would surely be wasted labour to trace the phrase 'trepido turbante tumultu' (literally, 'with fearful agitation disturbing [them]', line 15) to the various Virgilian contexts that seem to generate it; and perhaps misplaced ingenuity to find significance (homiletic, perhaps?) in the fact that in line 35 the phrase 'ausi immane scelus'[35] echoes Virgil's 'ausi omnes immane nefas' in *A.* 6.624, where Virgil sums up his grim catalogue of miscreants in the depths of Tartarus. In lines 43 and 44 descriptions of Jahweh's anger resemble, respectively, those of Aeneas at *A.* 12.946 ('furiis accensus et ira': ablaze with rage and anger' – the sudden anger to kill Turnus) and Juno, fired up with wrath against the Trojans, at *A.* 1.50 'flammato . . . corde'. These might be thought poor role models. In line 57 the succinct but clearly Virgilian phrase 'exempta fames' (*A.* 1.216, 8.184) recalls meals enjoyed by the Trojans, but not really in conditions of famine. A more plausible example of contextual relevance than any of the foregoing is the allusion in line 68 'omnibus exhausti prope casibus, omnium egeni' ('almost worn out by all their misfortunes, and lacking everything') to another line in book 1 (599: here Aeneas is describing the Trojans' plight), which undergoes minimal change.[36]

As often, allusions are not confined to the *Aeneid.* There is 'hominumque boumque labores' from Virgil *G.* 1.118 in line 92 (it is also to be found in 104.53). In line 136 'indeploratis' recalls Ovid (*M.* 11.670), and in 134 'conubialia' Statius (*Thebaid* 5.112: again the relatively unusual word, and the place it occupies in the rhythm of the line, assist in the detection). His use of 'palla' ('mantle') for darkness in *Thebaid* 2.527 might have inspired its use (referring to dust) in the simile at line 53. One other writer should be

---

[35] Buchanan is unaware that classical poets do not allow a short vowel to stand before a word with initial s and one or more consonants. For this feature, see Green, 'Matters of metre', 57.

[36] Buchanan substitutes 'exhausti' for 'exhaustos', 'prope' for 'iam', and 'egeni' for 'egenos'.

mentioned: Catullus. It seems likely that line 17 'irrita ventosis ut dent prae-
scripta procellis' recalls his 'irrita ventosae linquens promissa procellae'
(64.59: from a poem in hexameters, a kind of miniature epic), though there
is also a case for citing Statius (*Achilleid* 1.960 'irrita ventosae rapiebant verba
procellae'); debate on such a point, though not in itself misconceived, would
be unfruitful. There is a certain double echo of Catullus in lines 13 and 84
of the paraphrase, in the words 'benefacta priora' ('former benefits'). This
phrase – occupying almost half of the hexameter line and tripping off the
tongue quite distinctively – occurs in the same form, and at the same position, in the first line of his poem 76. This is a poem about love, one that can
reasonably be included in the Lesbia cycle; and it is surprising that Buchanan, who in the paraphrases puts off completely the role of the salacious
poet of love that he wears in many an epigram, recalls it in this context. But
the poem is open to a Christian interpretation: on the surface, at least,
Catullus is praying that the gods may recompense him for his kindness and
other good deeds, and although different interpretations are certainly possible,[37] especially now that approaches to ancient religion are more autono-
mous, it is a sentiment that a Christian Humanist – replacing the plural gods
with the singular – might have valued and echoed in his own relationships
to God and his fellow men.[38] One might even wonder if personal disappoint-
ment, or a sense of betrayal, helped fix it there.

PSALM 85

This psalm is essentially an appeal to God's kindness, and a prayer that his
wrath will be turned away. It touches on other themes appropriate to an epic
treatment – in lines 9 and 10, for example, where divine deeds from the past are
remembered – but it is not obvious why the hexameter metre was used, especially as it is a short psalm. In fact, its opening lines strike the tone of lyric:

> Non semper tumidis fervent vexata procellis
> aequora nec gelida riget horrida terra pruina:
> inque vicem ponunt venti, mare sternitur, aura
> mitior in florem torpentes evocat herbas.
> nec semper, deus, avertis maerentibus aurem . . .

[Not always do the seas boil, stirred by swelling storms, nor does the rough
earth stay rigid with chill frost; and in their turn the winds subside, the
sea is made calm, a gentler breeze calls the sleeping grasses into flower.
Nor do you continually turn your ear away from those who mourn, O
God . . .]

---

[37] See J. Booth, *Catullus to Ovid: Reading Latin Love Elegy* (Bristol, 1999), 25–32.
[38] Compare the suggestion made in Green, 'Davidic psalm', 96 about Horace, *Odes* 3.16.

Compare the beginning of a Horatian ode (2.9):

> Non semper imbres nubibus hispidos
> manant in agros aut mare Caspium
>   vexant inaequales procellae
>   usque, nec Armeniis in oris
> amice Valgi, stat glacies iners . . .

[Not continually do the rains pour into muddy fields from the clouds or uprooting storms harass the Caspian sea, nor, my friend Valgius, in the regions of Armenia does the ice stand motionless.]

The first two lines of the paraphrase render Horace's opening stanza in simpler words, without his unusual and exotic adjectives, and then, in lines 3 and 4, Buchanan makes a more positive point, still in lyric vein, before beginning his rendering of the psalm. Then, where Horace goes on to argue that Valgius should not keep up his lamentation for his deceased friend, Buchanan argues that God should not maintain his anger. Why, one asks, did Buchanan not use Horace's Alcaic metre? Since the nearest paraphrases in this metre are Psalms 82 and 91, and since it is one that he commonly uses, their relative proximity cannot be the reason. The answer must lie in the end of the poem. Lines 26–34 are as follows:

> Ecce salus, ecce **incultas** bona copia terras
> incolet, et laeti renovatrix gloria saecli.
> en bonitas, en alma fides feret obvia gressus;
> terra fidem, **caelo terras Astraea relicto**
> sancta colet; comes Astraeae **Bona Copia** caelo   30
> appluet, et laetos decorabit frugibus agros,
> et quacunque feret Dominus vestigia, gressus
> ante ferent ius fasque suos; lis visque dolusque
> deseret afflictas per tot iam saecula terras.

[Behold salvation, behold abundance will inhabit the untilled lands, and the renewing glory of a joyful age. Lo, goodness, lo, gentle honesty will bring their steps to meet us; the earth will cherish honesty, and holy Astraea leaving heaven will cherish the earth; abundance, the companion of Astraea, will rain down from heaven, and grace the fertile fields with fruit. And wherever the Lord takes his steps, law and righteousness will take theirs before him: strife, violence and deceit will desert the lands afflicted for so many centuries already.]

Vulgate:

10. verumtamen prope timentes eum salutare ipsius, ut inhabitet gloria in terra nostra.
11. misericordia et veritas obviaverunt sibi, iustitia et pax osculatae sunt.
12. veritas de terra orta est, et iustitia de caelo prospexit.
13. etenim dominus dabit benignitatem, et terra nostra dabit fructum suum.
14. Iustitia ante eum ambulabit, et ponet in via gressus suos.

In lines 29 and 30 we have a reference to Astraea, the maiden identified with Justice, who in classical mythology is said to have left the earth in disgust. The most famous reference to her return is in the so-called Messianic eclogue of Virgil (4.6 'iam redit et virgo': 'already the maiden returns'),[39] but she is also mentioned, and by name, in a few other places, among them Ovid's description of the ages of mankind early in his *Metamorphoses* (1.150): 'terras Astraea reliquit' ('Astraea left the earth'). The wording shows that Buchanan has this passage in mind, but he adds the epithet 'sancta', perhaps as a kind of disinfectant (like 'sancte' at 18.35; page 63). Her companion, Abundance, here is also Ovidian: in *M.* 9.87–8 'Bona Copia' creates the mythical 'cornucopia', the horn of the defeated Achelous, which was filled with fruits. Buchanan has brought these Ovidian passages together, and combined them with Virgil's optimistic reversal; in this he was surely influenced by the biblical personification in 'Iustitia de caelo prospexit'. The cornucopia in Horace's *Carmen Saeculare* (lines 59–60) may also have a role, for there it is accompanied by various virtues – though not Buchanan's 'bonitas' and 'fides', or the biblical 'misericordia' and 'veritas' to which they correspond – and indeed 'neglecta virtus' ('neglected virtue'), which recalls the neglect of justice that so offended Astraea.

A line of Virgil's fourth eclogue (29) also explains 'incultas' in line 26: the fields are untilled because they need no human labour to make them productive. One could talk of a pastoral ambience here, since it is from one of his pastorals that the Virgilian colour comes; but Virgil began this poem by declaring that he would sing of greater things. What Buchanan's poem provides is not so much a pastoral poem in the strict sense as a poem imaginatively derived from various sources, full of the sense of the beauty and bounty of nature so pervasive in Augustan verse.

PSALM 89

There is no doubt about the reason for the hexameter here, since this long psalm includes the themes of divine power, human kingship, warfare, and

---

[39] There is no need here to see a reference to the Virgin Mary, who is understood as the 'virgo' by those who found a prophecy of Christ's birth in this poem, simply because Mary can in no sense be said to have returned; Buchanan will have realised this.

wrath; and it has a wide historical sweep. But the dominating theme – one to which there is no sustained parallel in classical epic – is that of God's covenant with Israel, which Buchanan's Psalmist, again as 'vates', will make known. The first six lines are in many ways typical:

> Tu mihi carmen eris, rerum pater optime, semper,
> notaque erit populis bonitas, me vate, futuris,
> pollicitique immota fides, dum sidera mundo
> volventur tacito; citius quoque sidera credam
> in chaos antiquum lapso se condere mundo,
> irrita quam sacri credam fore foedera pacti . . .

[You will be my song, excellent father of all things, continually, and your kindness will be known to future peoples through me as your poet, as will the immovable trustworthiness of your promise, as long as the stars move through the silent universe; I could sooner believe that the universe will collapse and the stars bury themselves in primeval chaos than that the treaty of your sacred covenant could be of no effect . . .]

The whole poem is full of expressions of stability, permanence, and eternity. There are frequent instances of the classical figure known as the 'adynaton', by which the continuation of something of great worth – such as (in Virgil) love, fame, or some institution – is assured by linking the thought of its cessation with something deemed impossible. In epic they are often linked to the notion of Rome's eternity, but Buchanan's are based on the permanence of the created world. Although the word 'immota' in line 3 has some claim to be a favourite word of Virgil's, this poem is not memorable for its epic diction, until lines 71–6:

> Quippe semel sancto firmavi foedere, iurans
> per me, **nulla dies** initi cum Davide pacti
> **immemorem arguerit**: suboles, dum saecula mundus
> volvet, ei patrii sceptri moderamen habebit.
> **esto mi sol testis ad haec**, et conscia luna,
> cum quibus aequaevum sceptrum Iudaea tenebit.

[Indeed I have once confirmed it with a holy covenant, swearing by myself, 'No day will show me unmindful of the pact that I have entered with David; his offspring, while the world rolls the ages onward, will hold the governance of the ancestral sceptre for him. Let the sun be my witness to this, and the knowing moon, with whom Judaea will hold power of equal duration.]

The words 'nulla dies initi cum Davide pacti / immemorem arguerit' ('no day will prove me unmindful of the pact undertaken with David') recall a passage of Virgil from a different context (*A.* 9.281–2): 'me nulla dies tam fortibus ausis / dissimilem arguerit'. This is immediately followed at line 75 by 'esto mi sol testis ad haec . . .': ('let the sun be my witness on this . . .'), strikingly close to Virgil *A.* 12.176 'esto nunc Sol testis et haec . . .', where Aeneas swears to abide by the conditions of the imminent duel. It may be relevant that neither oath was justified in the sequel: Euryalus was brave, but ineffectual, and the solemn arrangements for the duel came to nothing. But God's mind was not changed: in line 48 he declared 'nulla meam vertet sententia mentem' ('no opinion will change my mind') (cf. *A.* 1.260: this is used also for Psalm 132). The contrast may be significant. One could claim a similar 'Kontrastimitation' in lines 32–3 'O terque quaterque / felices quos festarum clangore tubarum / ad tua sacra vocas' ('thrice, four times happy are those whom you call to your sacred rites with the clangour of festive trumpets'), where the initial phrase (Virgil *A.* 1.94, with 'beati') combines with a recollection of the Virgilian 'clangorque tubarum' (*A.* 2.313, 11.192). The trumpets which call to battle in Virgil (and in particularly upsetting contexts) call to joyous worship in their new context. It is possible to claim an instance of such 'Kontrastimitation' that proceeds in the opposite direction, at line 108, where the phrase 'circum innumerae gentes' (they are a 'profana turba', and behave like one) recalls a more optimistic context at *A.* 6.706.

But allusions are otherwise not frequent nor significant. In line 94, 'quem finem dabis aerumnis?' ('what end do you give to our sorrows?'), it seems as if Buchanan is consciously avoiding the similar Virgilian expression of *A.* 1.241 'quem das finem, rex magne, laborum?', which he might have used. In line 82 'gelida formidine' recalls Virgil *A.* 3.259 'gelidus formidine', but this combination of words is often, one might almost say routinely, used by Buchanan for feelings of fear. More interesting are his uses of two conspicuous words from outside epic: Horace's 'illacrimabilis' ('pitiless': *Odes* 2.14.6) in line 102 and the word 'revolubilis' (with 'mundi') in line 24, from the scientific writer Manilius (1.330: 'the revolving world'). Manilius was one of the less frequently read classical poets, and his presence may surprise until one realizes that Buchanan was very interested in such matters, which eventually led to his erudite astronomical poem *Sphaera.*[40]

This paraphrase, and those of Psalms 78 and 85, are less strikingly epic in character than those of Psalms 18 and 45. It may or may not be significant that these three all occur in a single book (book 3) of the Psalms, but it does seem that Buchanan has now decided to be more generous with the hexameter metre, which he denied (for example) to Psalms 21, 29, 65, and 68 in spite of their apparently promising subject matter. He does not restrict it to

---

[40] Both these words, as it happens, occur in Ausonius (13.8.3 and 14.1.12 respectively), but as these are little known poems they are unlikely to have been Buchanan's source. For Buchanan's *Sphaera*, 'which may go back to the 1540s', see McFarlane, *Buchanan*, 355–78.

poems which give an opportunity to parade his mastery of epic idiom and allusion and which are obvious candidates, though there are such among the remaining poems to be studied.

PSALM 104

The paraphrases of Psalms 104 and 107, both of which are in hexameters, may be seen as the first and last items in a small series, broadly homogeneous in theme and more or less equal in length; the fact that the fifth and final book of the Psalms begins at 107 may conceivably have influenced the choice of metre. Psalm 104 is a meditation on God's careful management of his world, as shown first in its restoration after the flood, and then in the economical regulation of its various components. The idea of majesty is prominent, especially near the beginning and the end, in lines 2 and 74, but not pervasive: the first of God's titles is 'Deus alme' (this suggests 'gentle', 'kind', 'supportive'), which sets a minor key. The firmament is like a tent (line 6), and although God rides on the clouds and the winds, as in Psalm 18, the 'wings of the wind' are light ('levibus') and the clouds which God guides like fast chariots are flitting ('volitantia'). Where the power and command of God are concerned, the tone briefly attains the level of epic: line 15 begins with 'increpuit', the following line with 'insonuere', and these typical and typically positioned verbs are followed by the distinctively Virgilian 'cernere erat' (*A.* 6.596, 8. 616). But once normality is restored to the world, we find (22) the 'liquidi fontes' ('clear springs') of the *Georgics* (4.18), and although the 'trackless rocks' mentioned by Virgil in the context of Aeneas' shipwreck (*A.* 1.537 'invia saxa'; cf. 25 'saxa invia') may be claimed as epic, they are here the haunt of the 'onager' (wild ass), a beast from his *Georgics* (3.409). At the end of the section there are pastoral notes, as the birds 'frequent their homes in the green branches, and soothe lonely places with their complaints'. The first verb, 'concelebrant', comes from Lucretius (2.345: see also below), while the melodious 'complaints' of the birds recall Virgilian and later pastoral.

The poem's central section begins (line 29) with a statement that is remarkably rich intertextually:

> Tu pater aerios montes camposque iacentes
> nectare caelesti saturas, fecundaque rerum
> semina vitales in luminis elicis oras.

[You, father, satisfy the lofty mountains and the low-lying plains with heavenly nectar, and bring into the lifegiving realms of light the fertile seeds of things.]

Vulgate:

rigans montes de superioribus suis; de fructu operum tuorum satiabitur
terra.

[watering the mountains from his higher resources (?); from the fruit of
your works the earth will be satisfied]

A specific origin in the classical poets may be identified for almost every
phrase here.

The 'celestial nectar' which satisfies, or indeed satiates, the mountains
('aerios' is common in epic) and the low-lying plains – Buchanan's phrase is
matched exactly in Lucan 4.52 – is probably derived from Ovid *M.* 4.252–3,
where Ovid describes the growth of the frankincense plant from the body of
Leucothoe: 'imbutum caelesti nectare corpus / deliciut', 'her body, soaked
with celestial nectar [the fragrance of the plant that grows in its place],
melted away'. This unusual passage was evidently preferred as a model to the
more celebrated one from the *Georgics* (2.325–7), with its sexual metaphor
of the god descending into the lap of the earth, an image which Buchanan
may have felt unsuitable; other allusions in this passage justify the speculation that he also had in mind a passage of Lucretius (2.333–80), its philosophical framework notwithstanding (the context is the variety of atoms),
and an earlier passage in Ovid on the earth's (re-)creation of animal life (*M.*
1.416–37). The words 'semina' and 'vitales' are reminiscent of Lucretius,
who uses them frequently, but Buchanan's 'fecunda rerum semina' ('fertile
seeds of things') do not behave like Epicurean atoms; it is better to compare
Ovid *M.* 1.419, less technical and verbally more exact. The phrase 'in luminis
oras' was also used a number of times by Lucretius (and appears prominently
in 1.22, in his invocation, as does 'genitabilis' at 1.11, which is used by
Buchanan a few lines later, at line 37), but an affinity with the *Georgics* – it is
accompanied in *Georgics* 2.47 by the word 'infecunda' ('infertile'), of weeds
which grow of their own accord – should also be noted.[41] It seems that
Buchanan considered a variety of passages, and here at least in view of his
broad range of demonstrable reading the attempt to specify particular
models in every case may be misleading.

The next section, too long to quote and in any case less intensely classical,
is conspicuous for its Georgic material. Note 'pabula' ('fodder': ten times in
the *Georgics*, though common in Latin generally), and 'faenum' (compare
'faenilia' ('haylofts': *G.* 3.321) for animals, with 'olus' ('cabbage': *G.* 4.130;
its presence in an explicitly humble context at Ovid *M.* 8.647 does not demonstrate epic status, but in this context the reverse) and its adjective 'genialis'
('enjoyable') in 33, for mankind, along with corn, wine and oil in the following lines. The trees offer lodging for the stork's 'fetus . . . implumis' (its still

---

[41] It is also found in Virgil *A.* 7.660, but with 'sub' for 'in'. The history of this fascinating phrase goes back
to Ennius.

unfeathered brood: *G.* 4.512–13). But the psalm's picture is in some ways more inclusive than that of the *Georgics*; the night allows wild animals to appear, such as the young lion ('leunculus'), in line 49.[42] This animal is described as 'praedator'; and this descriptive epithet, rarer than modern English 'predator' – Ovid and Statius use it, in their epics, of the eagle and tiger respectively – is neatly followed by its even rarer feminine form in the phrase 'praedatrix turba' ('predatory crowd'). Then, by day, emerges man, who, in the words of the Authorized Version, 'goeth forth unto his work and to his labour until the evening'; Buchanan's rendering of this recapitulates and reinforces his predominantly Georgic presentation of the created world with the phrases 'hominumque boumque labores' ('the works of men and oxen') from *G.* 1.118 (he uses this also at 78.92) and a slightly changed[43] version of the exquisite line 'illic sera rubens accendit lumina Vesper' (*G.* 1.251: 'there reddening evening lights its late lamps').

The next section, about the sea, is more difficult to characterize, though the language is certainly poetic. Its closing line (72) 'et desolatas gens incolit aurea terras' ('and a golden race inhabits the empty lands') combines Ovid ('desolatas . . . terras': *M.* 1.349) and Virgil ('gens aurea': *E.* 4.9). Claims for an epic register cannot be built on the compound adjectives 'squamigerae' (60: 'scale-bearing, scaly': sometimes in Latin a sort of kenning for 'fish') or 'veliferas' (62: 'sail-bearing': a word used in a variety of poetic genres); but in 77 the pedigree of the adjective 'fumifera' ('smoke-bearing, smoky') is distinctively Virgilian (*A.* 8.255 and 9.522), and so appropriate to the description of God's terrifying power in lines 75–7. This return to epic earnestness is matched in the attitude of the poet, who insists (line 78) that he will praise the Lord as long as he lives, 'dum spiritus hos regit artus' ('as long as breath governs these limbs'), unmistakeably recalling Aeneas' promise to Dido at *A.* 4.336.

PSALM 107

This psalm begins by praising God as 'dominumque bonum facilemque parentem' ('good lord and kindly parent'), a tone struck near the end of his version of Psalm 104 (line 79), and the psalm's main theme is God's kindness towards his chosen people. The summary description of their restoration, in lines 6–10, is coloured by a neat and verbally precise recollection of the wanderings of Aeneas and his followers: 'inhospita saxa' (*A.* 5.627). They have been rescued from the ends of the world, described by Buchanan in terms of the daily journey of the sun ('Phoebus' in line 8), who 'rises from

---

[42] This word is actually not found in classical Latin; dictionaries refer to other locations in the Vulgate, and so it will have come to Buchanan from his reading of other parts of the Old Testament, or perhaps through an intermediate neo-Latin source.

[43] The changes are syntactical: for 'illic' he has 'donec' ('until'), and this requires the subjunctive 'accendat'.

the waves' and 'buries himself in the waves', and as extending from the cold of the Arctic Bear[44] to the warmth of the south.

The poem is divided into sections by a most unusual system of refrains, corresponding to repeated verses of the psalm, a feature which has no parallel in classical epic[45] but which is given some epic colouring. As will be seen from the quotation below, there is a regular refrain of two lines, beginning 'ergo canant...' and echoing the praises of the first line of the psalm, at lines 17–18, 30–1, 42–3, and 61–2 (the last third of this poem has no refrains), and a subsidiary refrain, or leitmotif, of three lines, which, with some verbal variation, is worked into the sections which result. This occurs at lines 13–15, 25–7, 37–9, and 56–8, and includes epic touches in 'audiit' (lines 14 and 26: cf. page 63) the long word 'imploravere' (Ovid *M.* 8.269), and the distinctively (though not exclusively) Virgilian line ending 'egenos' (cf. page 69: *A.* 1.599). This and other aspects of the poem may be illustrated by a quotation of lines 46–63, which deals with 'those that go down to the sea in ships, that do business in great waters':

> Qui mare fluctisonum sulcat, curvisque carinis
> admovet externas vaga per commercia gentes,
> non ignota illi divina potentia, nec quae
> monstrat in immenso miracula saepe profundo.
> cum iubet, irrumpunt venti **stridente procella**, 50
> et mare nunc spumis canentibus **astra lacessit**
> et nunc **tartarei** subsidit ad ima **barathri**;
> pallent ora, metus trepidantia pectora pulsat.
> et velut oppressis vino vestigia nutant,
> callida nec **cani** iuvat ars aut cura **magistri**. 55
> at Dominum ut maestis **imploravere** querelis,
> exaudit trepidos et opis miseratus **egenos**;
> iam venti ponunt, strataque aequaliter unda,
> arrident taciti tranquilla silentia ponti.
> iam posita leti gaudent formidine nautae, 60
> cum **lacerae** optatum **portum tetigere carinae**.
> ergo canant Dominumque bonum, facilemque parentem;
> et late ignotis pandant facta inclita terris.

[The man who ploughs the wave-resounding sea, and in his curved ships visits foreign races with his roving trade, he is not unaware of the divine power, or of the miracles that God often shows in the immense deep.

[44] Since the Latin word 'Arctous' is closely related to the Greek word for bear ('arktos'), this is a play on words; Virgil treats Greek names in a comparable way, for example in *A.* 3.693, when he applies the epithet 'undosum' ('wave-tossed') to the place Plemmyrium, named after the Greek word for 'tide'.

[45] In Virgil *E.* 8 and later poems, a single-line refrain, grammatically unrelated to what surrounds it, breaks into the narrative or marks off individual sections; this feature is not closely parallel.

When he commands, the winds rush in with a howling storm, and the sea now challenges the stars with its white spray, now descends to the depths of Tartarus' pit; their faces are white, fear pounds their panicking hearts, and their footsteps totter as if they were drunk with wine; nor does the astute skill or the diligence of the old steersman help. But when they called upon the Lord with their sad complaints, he heard them in their panic, and pitied those who needed his help. Now the winds are stilled, and with the waters evenly[46] smoothed, the peaceful quiet of the silent sea smiles upon them. Now losing their fear of death[47] the sailors rejoice, when their damaged ships have reached the longed-for harbour.

Therefore let them sing of the good Lord, and their kindly parent, and let them reveal his famous deeds to unknown lands far and wide.]

There is a pivotal 'howling storm' early in Virgil's narrative (*A.* 1.102 'stridens . . . procella': cf. 50), but in representing the biblical storm Buchanan shows a notable desire to avoid the obvious. The picture of the waves hitting the stars at one moment and sinking to hell the next is actually close to the description of Scylla and Charybdis at *A.* 3.420–3, but Buchanan goes for variation, writing 'astra lacessit' in 51 (Lucan 10.320 may have suggested this) rather than using 'sidera verberat' from Virgil (line 423), which he might have worked in. At line 52, although Virgil (in *A.* 3.412) had used the word 'barathrum' in this rather unusual sense of 'the deeps', Buchanan alludes to a similar context in *Thebaid* 9.503 ('sidit crescitque barathrum': 'the deep subsides and rises up') and takes the adjective 'tartarei' from *Thebaid* 1.85, where it is used with 'barathrum' in a different sense. A similar combination of two passages occurs again at 61 'cum lacerae optatum portum tetigere carinae' ('when the damaged ships reach the longed for harbour'): the last three words occur at Virgil *G.* 1.303 – in an analogy that moves the reader momentarily from the agricultural world to the nautical – but are joined by the adjective 'lacerae', which is found with 'carinae' at Lucan 8.755. Buchanan could also have given Virgilian colour to the motif of the steersman's skill being useless (55) by recalling the storm at *A.* 3.201–2, a little earlier in their travels, but chooses not to do so; there is here a rare trace of Juvenal, the satirist and occasional parodist of epic, in the word 'cani' (12.32).[48]

---

[46] This may be understood in terms of the word 'inaequales' in the passage of Horace quoted at 71; although (as was observed) he simplified Horace's adjective 'inaequales' there, here he imaginatively devises a corresponding sense for the adverb 'aequaliter'.

[47] 'Leti' could also be translated 'joyful' or 'joyfully', but this would be blatantly tautologous. Many early versions have the spelling 'lethi', which indicates the word 'letum' ('death') that was so spelt because of confusion with 'lethe', the river of the underworld (whence English 'lethal').

[48] In his commentary, *A Commentary on the Satires of Juvenal* (London, 1980), 521, E. Courtney briefly notes the epic tone of the phrase 'prudentia cani / rectoris' ('the wisdom of the grey-haired steersman').

The final section, which describes the power of God to irrigate the desert or to dry up fertile lands, and, by extension, to give or withhold gifts, shows a wide variety of register, and indeed sounds an uncertain note. Classical diction is used to point up the distinction of wet and dry – the streams ('rivi') are 'bubbling' in 66 ('bullantibus': cf. Calpurnius Siculus 1.11),[49] 'fleeing' or 'fugitive' in 72 ('fugacibus': cf. Horace *Odes* 2.3.12) and the sand is infertile ('male pinguis harenae', Virgil *G.* 1.105). The rare verb 'fecundo' ('make fertile') from Virgil *G.* 4.293 is used, but so too is (in line 69) the prosaic word 'sterilesco' ('become sterile').

PSALM 132

This is a prayer to God to remember the trials of his people, and a confident forecast of their prosperity. The particular focus is on the temple of Sion, and through this theme Buchanan detects and develops parallels with the *Aeneid*, to a degree that we have not seen since Psalm 45. There are echoes of other poems here,[50] and they are not without significance, but the unified series of allusions to the *Aeneid*, perhaps the boldest of his transcultural assimilations, is paramount. The opening lines offer hints of this: one is the word 'laborum', which Buchanan prefers – like many exegetes – to the Vulgate's 'mansuetudo' (kindness), often used in the *Aeneid* of the trials of the Trojan refugees, and another is the phrase 'rebus egenis' (*A.* 6.91), which also recalls their plight.

In line 10 Buchanan takes the opportunity to begin his series of topographical allusions and create a relationship between two sites of especial sanctity. He recasts a phrase of the biblical text from verse 6, 'invenimus eum in campis silvae' ('we have found it [the place for the temple] in the wooded plains'), so that it becomes 'inter saxa tamen *silvestribus* obsita *dumis*' ([God showed the place] 'among rocks overgrown with the thorns of the forest'). This recalls a Virgilian moment, where Evander has been describing the site of Rome long before the city was founded, and adverts to the numinous sanctity of the Capitoline hill, 'now golden, but then bristling with thorns of the forest' 'aurea nunc, olim *silvestribus* horrida *dumis*' (*A.* 8.348).[51] This allusive identification of the two locations prepares the way for Buchanan to elaborate the resemblance between the politico-religious missions of David and Aeneas in a rich pattern of sophisticated allusions, especially in the following passage (lines 23–32):

---

[49] The beginning of Calpurnius' first eclogue appears also in the paraphrase of Psalm 23; see Green, 'Davidic psalm', 95–6.

[50] In line 20 'pectore puro' ('with a pure heart') recalls Horace, *Satires* 1.6.64, and in line 32 the phrase 'caeli indulgentia' recalls Virgil *G.* 2.345 (in a different sense, that of springtime).

[51] The adjective 'silvestribus' is found in the translation of Froschoverus, for the Vulgate's 'silvae' ('of the forest'), and could have sown the idea in his mind.

Davidi enim quondam (neque iam **sententia vertet**
ulla tuam mentem) iurasti: e stirpe propago
nata tua solium et sceptrum retinebit avitum.   25
quod si posteritas servet mea foedera, pactis
si steterit, leges si non temerarit avitas,
nulla dies **solio**, vis nulla extrudet **avito**,
et natos natorum, et qui nascentur ab illis.
ipse mihi sedem elegi **sine fine** Sionem,   30
quam colerem: hic mihi **certa quies**, hic certa voluptas,
haec mihi grata domus . . .

[For you once swore to David (and no other opinion will now change your mind): the race born of your stock will hold your ancestral throne and sceptre. If posterity keeps my covenant, and stands by our pact, if it does not infringe the ancestral laws, no day, no force will drive them from the ancestral throne, or the sons of their sons, or those who will be born from them. I myself have chosen Sion as my abode, for me to inhabit without end; here is my fixed place of rest, here is my fixed pleasure, this is my acceptable home . . .]

Vulgate:

11. Iuravit Dominus David veritatem, et non frustrabitur eam. de fructu ventris tui ponam super sedem tuam.
12. si custodierint filii tui testamentum meum, et testimonia haec quae docebo eos, et filii eorum usque in saeculum, sedebunt super sedem tuam.
13. quoniam elegit Dominus Sion, elegit eam in habitationem sibi.
14. haec requies mea in saeculum saeculi; hic habitabo, quoniam elegi eam.

In line 28 the 'ancestral' throne of the Jews is referred to by the words 'solio . . . avito', from Virgil *A*. 7.169, where they occur at the same positions in the hexameter, and so, through the word 'avitus' ('ancestral'), an important one in this paraphrase (it is used also at 25, 27, and 38, in this last case again with 'solium'), Buchanan makes a further link with the beginnings of Rome, or more precisely the Trojan/Latin/Italian amalgam from which Rome was to grow. It is tempting to go further and link this throne with the temple of Latinus, described by Virgil in the lines immediately following the one just quoted above, and pictured by him in various ways which recall the Roman Capitoline temple,[52] with the allusion to the Capitol hill in line 10;

---

[52] The detailed similarities are explained by W. A. Camps, 'A second note on the structure of the *Aeneid*', *Classical Quarterly* 53 (1959), 54 and in his book *An Introduction to Virgil's Aeneid* (Oxford, 1969), 56 and note 14.

but even if the point had occurred to him, Buchanan might not have chosen
to make the imaginative jump between these two localities in the way that
comes naturally to modern critics. A further link is made between the house
of David and the Roman race that is being established, by the appropriation
of a whole line, at line 29: 'et nati natorum et qui nascentur ab illis' (*A.* 3.98).
In Virgil this is part of an oracular response from Apollo in which the exiled
and homeless Trojans are told that the land they seek is one where 'the
house of Aeneas will rule over all shores, and the sons of their sons and those
who are born of them'.[53]

In another prophecy – and it is in keeping with the nature of the psalm
that Buchanan refers so often to prophecy – namely Jupiter's weighty prophecy near the beginning of the *Aeneid*, to which this paper has already referred
more than once, the Romans were promised dominion without end ('his ego
nec metas rerum nec tempora pono: imperium sine fine dedi': *A.* 1.278–9);
now in line 30 we find the same two words, 'sine fine'. In case the two words
'sine fine' are thought insigificant in themselves, the parallel is reinforced by
two further touches: Buchanan's 'ipse' corresponds to Virgil's emphatic 'ego'
(both mean 'I myself'), and in lines 23–4 Buchanan's Psalmist insisted
'neque iam sententia vertet ulla tuam mentem' in words that recall closely
words put into Jupiter's mouth in the same context: 'neque me sententia
vertit' (*A.* 1.260). Moreover, one should surely detect in the phrase 'hic mihi
certa quies' an echo of Virgil's 'requies ea certa laborum' (*A.* 3.393)[54] – part
of another prophecy – which points back to the word 'laborum' in the opening line. And this line of Virgil also refers to a specific location – the site of
Alba Longa, Rome's precursor on the Tiber – in the words 'is locus urbis erit'
('that will be the place for your city'), intensifying even further the sense of
place so carefully constructed in this poem.

There is yet one more relevant similarity, in line 41, where the Jewish race
is described as 'Iessaea propago'. The word 'propago' ('offspring' or more
generally 'posterity') is not uncommon in Buchanan, or in classical Latin,
but the Virgilian parallels should again be examined. In fact, he uses it
seldom, in any grammatical case, and only twice in the case-form 'propago',
at *A.* 6.870 and 12.827; the word 'Romana' precedes, immediately in the first
case. The first of these passages refers to the Roman race of Virgil's time,
fully developed though about to suffer a sad loss; the second is part of
Jupiter's prophecy at the end of the epic that the future Roman race will be
'strong with the manliness of Italy'. By inventing – it is not classical, at any
event – the adjective 'Iessaea' and creating a phrase which by its rhythm
and structure recalls Virgil on Rome, Buchanan neatly sums up the parallel
development of the two nations that he has been at pains to construct in
this poem.

---

[53] Also, in fact, a direct translation of Homer, *Iliad* 20.308.
[54] Manuscripts also give the line at *A.* 8.46, where the prophecies made in book 3 are fulfilled.

PSALM 135

This short psalm begins with an appeal to guardians of the temple to praise the Lord: its main themes are creation (lines 8–16), conquest (17–31) and ridicule of rival gods (32–43). A final section, reflecting and recapitulating the opening lines, calls upon those who dwell in the holy temple of Sion to praise the Lord (44–8).

There are various echoes of epic language in the first section of the poem, ones of no great significance either in themselves or as part of a wider structure of association. The interjection 'eia', though colloquial and without the elevated tones of 'Alleluia', is not out of place: heroes are sometimes so addressed (Virgil *A.* 4.569 and 9.38). The word 'gaza', also found in epic (e.g. Virgil *A.* 1.119) but by no means exclusively there, is a happy synonym (line 16) for the Vulgate's 'thesauris' ('treasures'). The description of the clouds being suspended in the 'clear' air by their creator ('suspendit in aere') hints at Ovid's creation story ('pendebat in aere tellus', *M.* 1.12). Otherwise there are 'caecis . . . tenebris' ('impenetrable darkness'), 'de viscere terrae' ('from the bowels of the earth'), 'super aethera' ('in the air above'), and 'liquido aere' ('in the clear air'), phrases which are commonplace and would occur instinctively to a writer of Buchanan's *copia*.

The central section is a different matter, and although it does not bristle with 'kings and battles', there is enough to awaken a more elevated style. The first war to be mentioned is the punishment of Egypt. Pharaoh is a proud king: 'regemque superbum' (cf. *A.* 11.15, 'de rege superbo', of the tyrant Mezentius). The similarity is not an exact one, and it might be pointed out that in *A.* 1.21 the same words, in this case differently arranged, are used of Rome itself.[55] This is followed by a line of undoubted pedigree, in which Buchanan combines Virgil's 'qui . . . bibunt' (*A.* 7.715: 'and those who drink . . .', meaning the inhabitants of the area watered by a particular river) with 'septemflua flumina Nili', from Ovid *M.* 15.753, where the epithet of the delta is transferred to the whole river. In line 29 Buchanan goes out of his way once more to use, unaltered, another famous line from Virgil: *A.* 6.853 'parcere subiectis et debellare superbos' ('to spare the submissive and war down the proud'), in which Aeneas' father lays down the principles of Roman military aggrandisement, and applies the words to God himself, 'sancte parens rerum qui iusto examine nosti' ('holy parent of all things, who knows with just balance . . .'). In the second half of this line the single word 'examine' (rare in this sense) is enough to recall Jupiter's fateful weighing of the fates of the adversaries Aeneas and Turnus in a balance at *A.* 12.725,[56] at the crucial point of the conflict.

---

[55] In a now classic example of 'deviant focalisation': see D. Fowler, *Roman Constructions* (Oxford, 2000), 48.
[56] Derived from Homer, *Iliad* 22.209–13.

Jupiter examines their fates; Jahweh distinguishes between the submissive and the proud.[57]

The next section, which ridicules the enemy's gods, offers scope for satire. Virgil had referred briefly to 'omnigenumque deum monstra' in *A.* 8.698, decrying the Egyptian deities, but this is not used; neither is the satire of Juvenal (15) deploring the intense hatred to which Egyptian religious rivalries could lead. But in line 33 Buchanan borrows the phrase 'vana superstitio' from Virgil *A.* 8.187, where he had Evander, king of proto-Rome, explain that the rite being witnessed by Aeneas was not the result of 'vain superstition' but performed by them 'because they have been saved'. The mild satirical tone that Buchanan – a most accomplished satirist in his secular poems – achieves in this section owes something to the short staccato phrases in which the futility of sacrifice is articulated ('they have mouths, but speak not; they have ears and hear not . . .') but also something to the expansion of one member, in 'et patulas frustra nares iucundus odorum / halitus incursat' ('the pleasant breath of aromas enters their wide noses in vain'), for such enlarged nostrils are associated in ancient Latin verse with animals, or in one case men bitten by one of Lucan's famous snakes (Lucretius 5.1076, Virgil *G.* 1.376, Lucan 9.813). When he goes on to say 'may anyone who creates and worships such ludicrous idols live a life similar to his gods' ('O quisquis ludibria talia fingit / aut colit, ipse suis similis dis exigat aevum'), Buchanan is with impressive recall using an appropriately sarcastic phrase from Virgil (*A.* 10.53) 'exigat hic aevum',[58] where Juno is saying that, for all she cares, Aeneas may live a life inglorious and unarmed. Buchanan develops his point with relish; and it is likely that he is aware of a passage of Ausonius, where, in one of his letters to Paulinus deprecating his friend's evident decision to withdraw from human company and end their poetic correspondence, he expresses his feelings in a curse which calls down on the person responsible a life bereft of the joys of human interaction.[59] He too uses the phrase 'mentis inops' ('out of his mind') and the word 'egens' ('lacking'), and in similar positions in the hexameter.[60] Ausonius was an author well known in early sixteenth-century France, and in his time had been a proud citizen of Bordeaux, a city with which Buchanan had recently been associated.[61]

---

[57] A problem for Roman generals, and for literary critics, at least those who sympathize with victims, such as Turnus, in Virgil.

[58] From the second part of Virgil's line the words 'magna dicione' ('with great authority') are found in line 24 of this poem, where they combine with *A.* 1.622 'dicione tenebat', thus linking Belus, an early conqueror of Cyprus, with Og the king of Basan.

[59] Ausonius 27.21.63–72.

[60] For another link with these letters, cf. Ausonius 27.22.32, 'nec dedignare parentem' and Psalm 132.16 'neu dedignare penates'.

[61] McFarlane, *Buchanan*, 78–92.

PSALM 1

This paraphrase has been left until last because it poses a substantial problem. Why was the hexameter used here? The short first psalm, which compares the lives and future prospects of the righteous and the wicked man, seems to have none of the themes which have been seen to influence Buchanan's choice: there is no hero, in the conventional sense, and no sense of nationhood; there is relatively little anger or majesty in the presentation of God. No specific demands on vocabulary are made by the psalm, and for the important first word there is either 'beatus' or 'felix', each of them compatible with several metres. In its realization the paraphrase shows no seeking after specifically epic diction – the compound 'pestiferae' (line 2) is one of the most widespread of these compounds, and 'veridicus' (line 16) one of the least epic – and there is no detectable allusion to epic or any other kind of hexameter writing. The problem will be clearer if the Vulgate is quoted first:

1. Beatus vir qui non abiit in consilio impiorum, et in via peccatorum non stetit, et in cathedra pestilentiae non sedit;
2. sed in lege Domini voluntas eius, et in lege eius meditabitur die ac nocte.
3. et erit tamquam lignum quod plantatum est secus decursus aquarum, quod fructum suum dabit in tempore suo; et folium eius non defluet; et omnia quaecumque faciet prosperabuntur.
4. non sic impii, non sic; sed tamquam pulvis quem proicit ventus a facie terrae.
5. ideo non resurgent impii in iudicio, neque peccatores in concilio iustorum.
6. quoniam novit Dominus viam iustorum; et iter impiorum peribit.

[Happy is the man who has not departed in the counsel of the wicked, and has not taken a position in the way of sinners, and has not sat in the seat of pestilence; but his will is in the law of the Lord, and he will mediatate in his law day and night. And he will be like a tree which has been planted near running waters, which will give its fruit in season; and its leaves will not fall away; and all things that it does will be prosperous. Not so, not so are the wicked; but like the dust which the wind blows from the face of the earth. Therefore the wicked will not rise in the judgement, nor sinners in the council of the just. Because the Lord knows the way of the just; and the way of the wicked will perish.]

The paraphrase runs thus:

> Felix ille animi, quem non de tramite recto
> impia sacrilegae flexit contagio turbae;
> non iter erroris tenuit, sessorve cathedrae
> pestiferae facilem dedit irrisoribus aurem;
> sed vitae rimatur iter melioris, et alta   5

mente dei leges noctesque diesque revolvit.
ille velut riguae quae margine consita ripae est
arbor erit; quam non violento Sirius aestu
exurit, non torret hiems; sed prodiga laeto
proventu beat agricolam; nec, flore caduco   10
arridens, blanda dominum spe lactat inanem.
non ita divini gens nescia foederis, exlex,
contemptrixque poli; subito sed turbine rapti
pulveris instar erunt, volucri quem concita gyro
aura levis torquet vacuo ludibria caelo.   15
ergo ubi veridicus iudex in nube serena
dicere ius veniet, scelerisque coarguet orbem,
non coram impietas maestos attollere vultus,
nec misera audebit iustae se adiungere turbae.
nam pater aethereus iustorum et fraude carentum   20
novit iter, sensumque tenet; curvosque secuta
impietas fraudum anfractus scelerata peribit.

[Happy is he in mind, whom the wicked contagion of the sacrilegious
crowd has not turned away from the right path; (who) has not held (to)
the path of error, or, a sitter in the pestilent seat, given a ready ear to
scoffers; but he explores the path of the better life, and with profound
mind ponders the laws of God day and night (7). He will be like a tree
which has been planted on the edge of a well-watered bank; which the
Dog-star with its violent heat does not parch, which winter does not
wither; but prolific with its healthy produce it makes happy the farmer;
nor does it, smiling with (only) flowers that will die, cheat its unsuspecting
master with flattering hopes (11). Not so the race ignorant of the divine
covenant, (who are) lawless, despisers of heaven: but they will be like the
dust caught in a sudden swirl, which the light breeze raised by a passing
eddy whirls about like a plaything, in the empty sky (15). Therefore, when
the truth-revealing judge will come in the calm clouds to pronounce
judgement, and will convict the world of sin, wretched wickedness will not
dare to raise its sad face in his presence nor to join itself to the good
crowd (19). For the heavenly father knows the path of the just and of
those lacking sin, and understands their intentions, and sinful wickedness,
following the crooked windings of deceit, will perish.]

A conspicuous feature of the psalm is the two contrasting similes which
between them occupy almost one half of it. While keeping to this proportion, Buchanan takes the opportunity to develop each of these as extended
similes in the classical epic tradition – for although the simile may be used
from time to time by other writers, it is a quintessentially epic feature, one
of many that go back to Homer – and though not long by Virgilian standards,

the similes here are longer than the few that sporadically occurred in the foregoing psalms. Buchanan may have welcomed this opportunity, but they are hardly a sufficient reason for choosing the hexameter; the fact remains that the subject matter is very unusual for epic or the related genres, and it is probable that if he had been consistent with his general practice he would have chosen a less elevated metre, the similes notwithstanding. It may be that the similes appealed to him not as a criterion for choosing the hexameter but as a possible legitimation of a choice made for some other reason.

That reason, I suggest, was in essence a programmatic one, and his aim to make a statement of poetic intent in his opening poem. Paraphrasers have little opportunity to express their aims: introductions may not be read, and modesty is expected. The point of putting the hexameter first is not to parade expertise; it is not – if only because so often used in teaching, and so commonly found in reading – a difficult metre to compose in, and others present greater challenges. Part of his purpose may have been to make a dignified opening, but there are no obvious confirmatory signs of such an intention. More importantly, it is a statement that he will be using the hexameter, a point of some importance because, as explained earlier, the hexameter was not associated with psalm paraphrases. But as well as pointing up this innovation, it declares that Buchanan's entire Psalter will be metrically inclusive to an extent that most of his predecessors were not; and it implies that he will not eschew the commoner metres, as was done by his immediate predecessor, the highly experimental Jean Gagnay. This last point may have been at the forefront of Buchanan's mind when he began to compose, but as the delays to publication gradually lengthened and Gagnay's reputation quickly sank, it may have been lost from sight.

* * *

In fulfilling his programme, Buchanan draws upon a very wide range of classical writing. Virgil, not surprisingly, is predominant, especially the books of his *Aeneid* that narrate the travels to Italy and the arrival in Latium: 1, 3, 4, 6, 7, and 8. Some episodes had little to offer, such as the Sack of Troy (book 2) and the Funeral Games (book 5), but almost all books of his epic have been seen to contribute something, if only at the level of brief verbal allusion or stylistic parallel. The *Georgics* are used frequently where the context permits, the *Eclogues*, with one important exception, hardly at all. Other authors used are the epic writers Ovid, Lucan, and Statius; the many-sided Catullus and Horace; the didactic writers Lucretius and Manilius, but sparingly; the satirist Juvenal, fleetingly; and the later writers Ausonius and (I stretch a point here) Boethius.[62] This list may well err on the side of brevity.

---

[62] In Psalm 68, where the hexameter metre alternates with a metre that is in effect part of a hexameter, the first line recalls the incipit of the famous verse passage that follows *Consolatio* 3.9.

We need not assume that this range, and the detailed knowledge shown of all these passages, are solely the result of a capacious and efficient memory, in the service of a scholar who must have been a fluent reader, and who could read copiously and fast. No doubt Buchanan did remember a great deal of the authors that he read and studied, at whatever age, but he is surely likely to have noted down appropriate passages from his reading, both before he began and after getting started. Some of the evidence assembled above invites the speculation that he noted parallel passages on certain matters. Although a general impression of Buchanan is that he did not have the mind, or at least the inclination, of the commentator or textual critic, who more or less systematically amasses relevant material and carefully compares similar passages, it seems difficult to imagine that he did not research his paraphrases carefully. There is no need to downplay the possibility that he frequently looked things up, at least once the straitened circumstances imposed by the Spanish Inquisition were behind him; further research may well show that his considerable *copia* and understanding of the classics owed rather more to *Hilfsmittel* of some kind than this study, and its precursor, have assumed.

As well as the sheer volume, the versatility is impressive. Psalm 1, as we have seen, gave no hint of this, and was not designed to; but Psalm 18 is, or rather includes, a masterpiece of epic writing, inspired by many separate models. Its storm, which is not a destructive one as in the early books of the *Aeneid* and the *Thebaid*, but one that brings and typifies salvation, could be seen as in some sense Buchanan's own curtain-raiser. Psalm 45 concentrated on Virgil, and is closely focused; again, it is not the destructive love affair of the *Aeneid*, but a marriage of great significance. Psalm 132 is similar in its approach, and if anything more unified, as it develops parallels between the sacred spaces at the heart of each civilization and looks forward to the future of the 'Iessaea propago' by alluding to the Roman experience. Psalms 78 and 89 both stress the persona of the 'vates', but their writing is more independent, as the subject-matter – the wandering in the desert, and the establishment of the covenant – requires; they demonstrate what an accomplished user of this metre Buchanan was in his own right. His allusive range reaches out to other genres in Psalms 85 and 104, the former notable for its lyrical and almost pastoral touches, the latter strongly Georgic. In Psalm 107 we see, within epic, more examples of a trend to avoid the obvious; in 135 the satirist briefly succeeds the epicist.

Compared with the previous paper on Buchanan's Horatian poems, this one has focused less on philosophical issues, and what may be called in a broad sense stylistic matters have been more dominant. Philosophical matters – whether ethical, ideological, or theological – are not irrelevant or inconspicuous in the epic context, but there were fewer pitfalls for Buchanan, and indeed a wider choice. At the theological level, there was no great problem, provided that he kept to a monotheistic conception – but at 89.11

and 16 he makes references to a 'companies' ('coetus') of higher beings, closely based on verses 4 and 5 of the psalm – and to the supposedly supreme Jupiter, airbrushed where necessary. Between these psalms and the *Aeneid*, there is also, at least in a general way, a notable convergence in ideology; a common concentration on the survival and success of a divinely led people through suffering, warfare, and conquest, which brought a high valuation of military virtues, a strong respect for the religious practices of the state, and an admiration for public wealth and its public uses. This is, of course, the 'optimistic' *Aeneid*, to use that common term of twentieth-century scholarship, and he also uses the 'optimistic' *Georgics*. Buchanan would not deny the other side of the coin, and certainly does not ignore the strand of individual distress or ethical uncertainty so prominent in the psalms, but for these he tends to use the iambic metre. Because of their frequency, and the relative dearth of possible classical models, these paraphrases too promise an interesting investigation.

University of Glasgow

5

A spirit of literature – Melville, Baillie, Wodrow, and a cast of thousands: the clergy in Scotland's long Renaissance

ALASTAIR J. MANN

In his poem 'Caledonia', written in 1706, Daniel Defoe described Scotland as 'the first sister to the Frozen Zone'.[1] He was reflecting on what he regarded as the grim condition of Scotland and, in particular, his assessment of a nation as a cultural backwater. Is this a reasonable assessment of Scotland in the late medieval and early modern periods, and in those relatively belated decades we consider the Scottish Renaissance? In the first half of the sixteenth century Scotland delivered the writings of the academics John Mair, John Vaus, and Hector Boece, a group of authors who gained an international audience and access to international presses. In the same decades, the domestic press proved capable of the outstandingly printed, vernacular edition of Boece's *Hystory of the croniklis of Scotland* (*c.* 1540), printed by Thomas Davidson in Edinburgh and translated by the poet John Bellenden, archdeacon of Moray and canon of Ross. Thus Scotland was, in the general literary field at least, not without some cultural merit at this stage in its history. Was the 'zone' then subject to an ice age after the Scottish Reformation in 1560? Although Defoe was of Puritan sympathies, he judged Scotland's elite and clergy too obsessed with religious politics in the sixteenth and seventeenth centuries.[2] Studies of high politics and the historiography of the Scottish Church and State provide abundant examples of this national preoccupation.[3] Nonetheless, faith and church politics in the Calvinist citadel

---

[1] Daniel Defoe, *Caledonia: A Poem* (Edinburgh, 1706), 1.

[2] See Defoe's letters to Robert Harley, earl of Oxford, in 1706–7, and subsequent tracts on Scotland and Scottish affairs. G. H. Healey (ed.), *The Letters of Daniel Defoe* (Oxford, 1955), 125–212 and Defoe's *An Historical Account of the Bitter Sufferings and Mellancholly Circumstances of the Episcopal Church in Scotland* (Edinburgh, 1707), *passim.*

[3] Seventeenth-century observers such as the cleric James Kirkton and lawyers Sir John Lauder of Fountainhall and Sir George Mackenzie of Rosehaugh are selections from the early modern deluge of politico-religious writing. Modern historiography has generally followed suit even in thoughtful recent studies. See James Kirkton, *The Secret and True History of the Church of Scotland from the Reformation to the Year 1678* [*c.* 1693], ed. R. Stewart (Lewiston, NY, 1993); Sir John Lauder of Fountainhall, *Historical Notices of Scottish Affairs, 1661–1688* (2 vols, Edinburgh, 1848); Sir George Mackenzie of Rosehaugh, *Memoirs of the Affairs of Scotland from the Restoration of King Charles II* (Edinburgh, 1821); and as a modern example, Alan R. MacDonald, *The Jacobean Kirk, 1567–1625: Sovereignty, Polity and Liturgy* (Aldershot, 1998).

of post-Reformation Scotland manifested many cultural dimensions, not least within the culture of print.

In many pre-modern but civilized societies the most learned, wise, and educated group are the engineers of public worship – the priests, ministers, monks, rabbis, and imams. The sixteenth-century clergy of Scotland, before and after the Reformation, was acutely engaged with learning and literate culture. Clerical involvement in the literature of the day, the mechanics of education at school and in the medieval college and monastery, the accumulation of books in libraries for personal and group instruction, and the development of contacts in the international sphere of ideas and knowledge, including education abroad, especially at Paris and Leiden, show the extent of that engagement. Moreover, the link with the book trade was especially close and symbiotic.[4]

The clergy was the most important nursery of budding authors in Scotland's medieval and early modern periods. The Reformation of 1560 changed little in that respect. After the Reformation, however, the church courts, from the General Assembly to kirk sessions, became very active publishers. Projects were of varied scale: large, such as the involvement by the wider clergy in the publication of and information gathering for the atlas of Scotland within Johan Blaeu's *Atlas Novus* (1654) and *Atlas Major* (1662), based on the cartography of Timothy Pont (*c.* 1565–*c.* 1614),[5] or deceptively small, as when the General Assembly in 1573 granted Richard Bannatyne a small grant to help with the editing of John Knox's *History of the Reformation in Scotland* (1586).[6] Local church courts became much exercised by liturgical printing, as when the Aberdeen presbytery and synod between 1683 and 1688 developed a complex plan to publish a new catechism, or in 1612, when the synod of Fife formed a committee to set down and have printed a short and clear Confession of Faith for the instruction of its parishioners.[7] Meanwhile, clerics both Episcopalian and Presbyterian became involved in the vast liturgical projects after the Reformation. The most significant of these complex programmes were those of the 1560s to set firm the liturgy of the Protestant church; the episcopal liturgical revolution from 1616 to 1637,

---

[4] For a discussion of the clergy and the book trade see Alastair J. Mann, *The Scottish Book Trade: Print Commerce and Print Control in Early Modern Scotland* (East Linton, 2000), 35–65; for a general summary of the book trade in Scotland see Mann, 'The anatomy of the printed book in early modern Scotland', *Scottish Historical Review*, LXXX/2 (2001), 181–200.

[5] For a summary of the historiography of Pont see Mann, 'The atlas of the 'Flemish priest': government, law and the publishing of the first atlas of Scotland', *Publishing History*, 50 (2001), 5–29. For the most recent overview see I. Cunningham (ed.), *The Nation Survey'd* (East Linton, 2002). The map library of the National Library of Scotland [NLS] has various editions of these atlases in various languages, including in Latin NLS, WD3B (1654) and WD3B (1662).

[6] David Calderwood, *The History of the Kirk of Scotland* (8 vols, Edinburgh, 1842–9), III, 276–7; A. Peterkin (ed.), *The Booke of the Universall Kirk of Scotland* (Edinburgh, 1839), 219.

[7] National Archives of Scotland [NAS], Aberdeen Presbytery Records, CH2/1/2, 428 and Minutes of the Synod of Aberdeen, CH2/840/10, 316; G. R. Kinloch (ed.), *Selections from the Minutes of the Synod of Fife, 1611–1687* (Edinburgh, 1837), 44–5.

when a complete new series of texts was introduced from the 'catechism' *God and the King* (1616); the 'King James Psalms' (1631), the Book of Canons (1635), and the controversial Service Book (1637); and also the Covenanters' uniform liturgy, which was created, after much consultation with England, between 1643 and 1650.[8]

But the clergy were individual as well as collective bibliophiles. The more wealthy and antiquarian made bequests of their libraries to posterity, as did James Boyd to Glasgow University in the 1620s or Bishop Robert Leighton (1611–84) to Dunblane Cathedral in the 1680s, the latter a wonderful collection that still exists today.[9] Patrick Galloway, minister of St Giles in Edinburgh, who died in the 1620s, left in his will a library valued at over £2500 Scots.[10] Typically such collections exhibited many books from the presses of Europe as well as Scotland. Thus the post-Reformation clerical reader of comfortable or modest means, Episcopalian or Presbyterian, became inextricably linked to the supply networks of printed books reaching out from Scotland to the rest of the British Isles and to Continental Europe. Book traders and faith promoters had the common interest in encouraging a culture of learning and private study, and the proliferation of printed texts. The link between trade and religion was remarkably close. The apprentice rolls of Edinburgh from 1583 to 1755 show over twenty sons of ministers apprenticed to the Edinburgh book trade, including individuals such as the printer John Wreittoun (apprenticed 1609), a member of the Presbyterian book trade network that existed long before the reign of Charles I, and the bookseller Alexander Ogstoun (apprenticed 1651), who, in the 1680s, imported English bibles into Scotland in breach of the right of Scotland's royal printer, the ubiquitous monopolist Agnes Campbell.[11] Faith and trade sometimes had scant regard for national boundaries.

What the clergy wrote as well as what they read provides the cultural historian with much food for thought when we consider the intellectual changes in the early modern period. A survey of the histories, memoirs, and correspondence of Scotland's early modern clergy can leave us with no doubt as to the level of individual erudition that could be achieved by clerics. The major literary figures – John Knox, James Melville, John Row, David Calderwood, John Spottiswoode, Robert Baillie, James Kirkton, Gilbert

[8] Mann, *The Book Trade*, 62–5.

[9] John L. Thornton, *The Chronology of Librarianship* (London, 1941), 168; W. J. Couper, *Bibliotheca Leightoniana Dunblane* (Glasgow, 1917).

[10] This was a large sum of money. From 1603 the exchange rate stabilized at £1 sterling to £12 Scots. W. Roland Foster, 'A constant Platt achieved: provision for the ministry, 1600–38', in D. Shaw (ed.), *Reformation and Revolution* (Edinburgh, 1967), 136–7; Mann, *The Book Trade*, 210.

[11] F. J. Grant (ed.), *Register of Apprentices of the city of Edinburgh, 1583–1666* (Edinburgh, 1906); C. B. B. Watson (ed.), *Register, 1666–1700* (Edinburgh, 1929) and *idem, Register, 1700–1755* (Edinburgh, 1929); James Watson, *The History of the Art of Printing* (Edinburgh, 1713), 16; Fountainhall, *Historical Notices*, II, 866; Mann, 'Book commerce, litigation and the art of monopoly: the case of Agnes Campbell, Royal Printer, 1676–1712', *Scottish Economic and Social History*, 18/2 (1998), 132–56.

Burnet, and Robert Wodrow – provide a fascinating, if hardly politically balanced, cross-section of men steeped in the world of clerical letters and contemporary religious controversy. Presbyterianism was, of course, intoxicated by its own triumphalism, and its greatest propagandist and most indispensable historian was David Calderwood (1575–1651). Nevertheless, perhaps the most compelling insight into a spirit of literature derives from the diaries and letters of James Melville (1556–1614), Robert Baillie (1602–62), and Robert Wodrow (1679–1734).

***

James Melville was born in 1556, son of Richard Melville, minister of Montrose in Angus. He was nephew and constant companion to Andrew Melville (1545–1622), the great Presbyterian divine who led the Presbyterian church party in the reign of James VI and did more than any other individual to establish a Presbyterian church structure. James Melville did not shine as brightly as his uncle as scholar/theologian, or politician, nor like Andrew did he travel, study, and teach on the Continent, but his *Autobiography and Diary* confirms his insight, intelligence, and unshakeable faith. The *Diary* was not actually printed until 1829, although it circulated in manuscript and came into the hands of Calderwood, who used it as a major source for his great *History of the Kirk of Scotland* (1679).[12] In the 1580s and 1590s Melville became minister of Anstruther-Wester and Kilrenny in Fife, but his views and association with his uncle led King James to commit both to prison in London in 1606. While Andrew was forced into exile, James was warded in Newcastle the same year and thence to Berwick-upon-Tweed in 1610, where he remained for the remainder of his life.[13]

James Melville's *Autobiography and Diary* reveals a man, in youth or maturity, devoted to scripture, the study of ancient languages, and even to the writing of sonnets. His childhood education in Montrose, starting in 1564/5, was carried out privately and at the local grammar school. His studies included not only the reading of 'catechism, prayers and scripture' but 'Latin Grammars, withe the vacables in Latin and Frenche . . . the Etymologie of Lilius . . . the Minora Colloquia of Erasmus', and the works of Virgil, Horace, and Cicero. Ancient history was absorbed. Later, and most significantly, the details of recent history were to be understood through reading 'Mr Bowchannan['s] Cronicle', Buchanan's controversial *Rerum Scoticarum Historia* (1582), and also the same author's politically explosive *De Jure Regni Apud Scotos* (1579).[14]

---

[12] James Melville, *The Autobiography and Diary of Mr James Melville*, ed. R. Pitcairn (Edinburgh, 1842). Caldewood acquired one of the most important manuscript editions and it passed down through his family. A simple comparison between the two books shows how Calderwood utilized some of Melville's recollections. See Melville, *Diary*, xxv.

[13] H. Scott (ed.), *Fasti Ecclesiae Scoticanae* (8 vols, Edinburgh, 1915–20), v, 212–3.

[14] Melville, *Diary*, 16–17.

Between enrolling as a student at St Leonard's College in St Andrews in 1571 and commencing as a regent of the University of Glasgow in 1575, teaching Greek, logic, and rhetoric, Melville recollects how his uncle Andrew Melville instructed him in more advanced studies – 'the Comentares of Caesar . . . Salust . . . the Conjuration of Catelin . . . Hebrew' and much else besides. Astronomy was also a passion for the younger Melville. When a 'strang meteor' shot through the sky in December 1604, he was able to comprehend the event and to recall his knowledge of astronomy gleaned from the writings of such as Tycho Brahe, Thaddeus Hagatius, and Paulus Fabricius. And yet, in spite of this 'proto-scientific' perspective, which existed in parallel with his faith, he conveyed a mixed response to an eclipse of the moon witnessed in 1597. At first, he rationalized it as a 'matter but commoune', but then fell to his knees 'prostrate in fear'.[15]

If a man of the education of James Melville can be so disorientated by fear and superstition, we have some indication of the anxious character of Scotland's early modern clerical readership. But, as corroborated by the extant productions of Scotland's presses of the sixteenth and seventeenth centuries, to which we must add imported books from the characteristic output of the presses of England and continental Europe, the predominant subject, for authors and readers, was God. Theology, scripture, and aspects of religious controversy, with advanced grammars and numerous classical authors, were the backbone to education at college, as well as the context for literary communication between brethren at home or abroad.[16] As for the sometimes dark aspects of nature which might defy educated understanding, the uncertain daylight of science had not yet been reached by the path of natural history. The decades from 1590 to 1720 were, after all, Scotland's 'age of witchcraft', and the most educated of kings, James VI, had even gone into print on the subject with his *Daemonologie* of 1597.[17]

The book supply environment in King James's reign, during which Melville acquired his education and developed his ideas about religion and politics, was essentially the first phase in the establishment of a permanent and sustainable domestic book trade for Scotland. Scotland had no formal incunabula period, printing not arriving until 1507–8, but it is reasonable to conclude that the years up to 1560 represent a similar early period when foundations were laid, materials imported, and skills learned. However, specialist booksellers began to appear (mainly in Edinburgh) only after the conclusion of the Marian Civil War in 1573, which saw the supporters of Mary, Queen of Scots either defeated or pacified by the followers of the infant King James. Peace allowed the growth of domestic and international book trading.

[15] Melville, *Diary*, 45–7, 525, 569–70.

[16] For the curriculum of Glasgow and St Andrews see Melville, *Diary*, 49; Calderwood, *History*, III, 339.

[17] See J. Craige (ed.), *Minor Prose Works of King James VI and I : Daemonologie; The True Lawe of Free Monarchies; A Counterblaste to Tobacco; A Declaration of Sports* (Edinburgh, 1982).

This first phase was, in the sense of domestic printing, concerned largely with the essentials of reading and education. It was a period, nonetheless, of mixed publishing, of the celebration of vernacular Scottish literature, from the poetry of Robert Henryson and William Dunbar to the patriotic epic verses of Wallace and Bruce, and of the provision of liturgy as well as school books and ABCs.[18] While some though not all of the pressure for the Reformation in Scotland came from the presses of England, by the 1570s regular channels of book trade communication had certainly been established. According to the 1579 testament of the Edinburgh printer/bookseller Thomas Bassandyne, London was then the source of eighty per cent of his English-language stock. For post-Reformation Scotland, English was the language of God. In fact, fifty per cent of the books imported from England between 1500 and 1625 were on theology, and the Puritan and Episcopalian controversies that swept through England were familiar to James Melville. Nevertheless, twenty per cent of the imports from England were practical guides indicating a new market for non-fiction and a developing thirst for more general knowledge. In Melville's time, English printers and stationers such as Richard Watkins, Richard Field, Robert Allott, and Godfrey Edmonson supplied the bulk of vernacular books to Scotland.[19]

Meanwhile, Latin theology, classics, and law texts, many so vital to the university years of Melville, came mainly from the Low Countries. In the 1570s and 1580s, Edinburgh booksellers such a Bassandyne and Henry Charteris were extensively supplied with Latin printings by Christopher Plantin of Antwerp, either as wholesale supplier or with editions from the Plantin press itself. An order made by Charteris to Plantin in July 1583 included the biographies of Socrates and Scipio, and the writings of Homer, Pindar, Horace, Virgil, Terence, and many other ancient writers, along with the works of Peter Ramus, Hebrew bibles, psalters, and grammars. The order included the 'Psalterium Buchanani', the famous psalm book composed by Buchanan and printed by Plantin himself, though also by numerous other presses throughout Europe.[20] The fall of Calvinist Antwerp in 1585 ended Plantin's direct Scottish trade, but the Low Countries continued to dominate Latin supply, especially out of Amsterdam. Many volumes from Holland and Northern Europe were imported by Andro Hart, the wealthiest Scottish printer/bookseller of the time. So it was that London and Edinburgh Latin printings were not very significant to Scottish readers and academics until the 1630s,

[18] For the output of the Scottish press in this period see Harry. G. Aldis, *A List of Books Printed in Scotland before 1700: Including Those Printed Firth of the Realm for Scottish Booksellers* (Edinburgh 1904, reprinted and updated 1970). For a summary see also Mann, 'Anatomy of the printed book', 185–7.
[19] Mann, *The Book Trade*, 225. D. Laing (ed.), *The Bannatyne Miscellany* (3 vols, Edinburgh, 1827–55), II, 191–204; F. S. Ferguson, 'Relations between London and Edinburgh printers and stationers to 1640', *The Library*, 4th ser., VIII (1927), 145–98.
[20] Museum Plantin-Moretus [MPM], Plantin Journals, no. 60, fol. 66'. For details on Plantin and Scotland see Mann, 'The book trade and public policy in early modern Scotland, c. 1500–c. 1720' (Ph.D., Stirling, 1997), 124–7.

which left Melville to look across the border for most English texts and across the North Sea for most Latin. Although, in his own youth, he marvelled at Robert Lekpreuik's Edinburgh/St Andrews press, seeing for the first time 'that excellent art of printing', and he witnessed in 1581 Alexander Arbuthnet's printing of the first edition of Buchanan's twenty volume *Rerum Scoticarum Historia*, Melville understood the limitations of Scotland's national press.[21] Scotland's expanding band of booksellers mattered more than a still small domestic press.

Compared with James Melville, the erudition of Robert Baillie and Robert Wodrow was even more impressive, but again they were driven by a personal quest for knowledge of the world and the continual replenishment of faith. Baillie was born in Glasgow in 1602, and for much of his life was associated with the same burgh. His father was a Glasgow merchant burgess of modest means. This did not hold back the son, however, and after grammar school Robert moved on to university in Glasgow, graduating M.A. in 1620. He proved himself a brilliant scholar, speaking a remarkable thirteen languages, even though, like Melville, he was educated solely in Scotland.[22]

Subsequently, as well as being appointed a regent of divinity at Glasgow, minister at Kilwinning in Ayrshire in 1625, one of the Westminster diplomat/divines that negotiated with England in the 1640s, and finally principal of Glasgow University in 1660, Baillie was a great bibliophile, ardent controversialist, and a committed literary agent. Letter wills produced by him in May and July 1639, and in October the following year, show that his private collection of books was valued at nearly £1400 Scots. Many of his book purchases, mostly from the booksellers of the Low Countries and London, were for the Glasgow college library. Nonetheless, in a plaintive cry familiar to many, he admitted in January 1643 to having spent too much money on his own books at the risk of building up alarming levels of personal debt. Baillie was also a considerable author. Although he wrote and published extensively, to a modern audience he is best know for his letters and journals.[23] These are an indispensable source for the historian and also provide a window to the complex mind of the man.

In the sphere of church politics, Baillie was, in the mid-1630s, something of a reluctant opponent of Charles I's ecclesiastical policies. He was always for moderation in all things and, though his life was disrupted by the turmoil of civil war, craved the quiet life. Indeed, the respect in which he was held and his thoughtfulness in the face of controversy made him an important person to win round. Baillie had the power to bring with him moderate opinion that increased support for the Revolution.[24] During the years of the

[21] Mann, *The Book Trade*, 71–3, 225, 228. Calderwood, *History*, III, 301–2; Melville, *Diary*, 28, 120–1.
[22] David Stevenson, *King or Covenant?: Voices from the Civil War* (East Linton, 1996), 17–39; *Fasti*, III, 116–7, 474.
[23] D. Laing (ed.) *The Letters and Journals of Robert Baillie* (3 vols, Edinburgh, 1842), I, 244, 267; II, 40.
[24] Stevenson, *King or Covenant?*, 21–2.

Covenanting regime he proved himself a defender of their cause. After 1650 he was clearly a member of the moderate Resolutioners faction, although this did not prevent his vitriolic personal letter to his most important patron John Maitland, second earl of Lauderdale, berating him for not preventing the 'neo-episcopalianism' of the Restoration.[25] The minister who wrote of the 1637 Service Book crisis 'It rests that we pray for a happie event to God, that he would avert the poperie on the one side, and the schisme of the other', and who, in August 1641, respected the ecumenicalism of John Durie's *Negotiation of peace among Protestants*, was, nevertheless, a devout Presbyterian who engaged in over twenty years of pamphlet combat in defence of his preferred form of church polity.[26] Scottish Presbyterianism was never sufficiently secure, at least before the eighteenth century, for its adherent authors not to take every opportunity to go into print.

Baillie adopted three methods of promoting Presbyterianism: publishing his own output, encouraging other Scottish divines and authors to enter the fray, and pressing for continental authors to express their support, mostly through his cousin William Spang, literary agent and minister at Veere (Scotland's staple port in the Low Countries) from 1630 to 1653. Baillie's letters and journals show a continual dialogue with Spang and others over the printing of his own works, the most significant of which were *The Canterburian's Self-Conviction* (Amsterdam and perhaps also London, 1640), published anonymously and revised by the leading Covenanter Archibald Johnston of Wariston; *Ladensium* (Amsterdam, 1640); *The Unlawfulness and Danger of Limited Episcopacie* (Edinburgh, 1641); *A Dissuasive from the Errors of the Time* (London, 1645); *Appendix Practica ad Joannis Buxtorsii Epitomen Grammaticae Hebraeae* (Edinburgh, 1653), the preface to which led to ripostes from James Veitch, and *Opus Historicum et Chronologicum* (Leiden, 1663). Each of these works produced a stream of replies and answers to replies. When, in early 1641, Baillie gleefully noted the fretful response of 'the adverse partie their Bishops and Doctors' to his *Canterburian*, he immediately had the work reprinted with an additional supplication. In another example of controversialism, Baillie delivered a retort to Dr John Bramhall's *A Fair Warning to Take Heed of the Scottish Discipline* with his *A Review of Doctor Bramble, Late Bishop of Londonderry, his Faire Warning against the Scotes Discipline*. Remarkably, both were printed in Delft in 1649. The printers of the Low Countries often put commercial before religious considerations.[27]

There are also many examples of Baillie encouraging and supporting the writings of other sympathetic authors. He repeatedly pressed Wariston to publish his own writings, as well as to license those of others, out of Wariston's responsibilities as Clerk to the General Assembly, a post he held from

---

[25] Baillie, *Letters*, III, 458, 459–60.
[26] *Ibid.* I, 14, 364.
[27] *Ibid.* I, 299; *ibid.* III, 87. Bramhall became archbishop of Armagh after the Restoration.

November 1638. In 1642 Baillie wrote to Wariston recommending that he publish his pamphlet *A New Letter to a Friend* '[for you] to enlighten and quicken us', and two years before, Wariston was asked to contact the young Henry Rollock, who had 'set down our proceedings to the pacification at Dunce', and to 'encourage him to put it to the press as it will doe us good over sea'.[28] In one of his numerous letters to Spang, this one dated 1644, Baillie stated that he 'like[d] well' the piece sent to him written by Mr [Patrick] Forbes in Delft, and that he 'wish[ed] it were in print', concluding – '[it is] good you keep correspondence with this young man'.[29] Sympathetic controversialists were induced to raise their pens. In February 1653, James Wood, professor of theology at St Andrews, was harangued to reply to a Nicholas Lockyer tract – 'will you let Lochier triump whole years?' – and a refutation was duly printed the following year.[30] Baillie never gave up the battle against the dark notions of sectaries, papists, Episcopalians, and even Remonstrants, the extreme faction of Covenanters which came to prominence after the Engagement crisis (1647–8) when nobles and moderates attempted to come to terms with Charles I.[31]

One of the most significant conduits for the publishing of Scottish clerical tracts in the years of Covenanting and Cromwellian government was the channel, astonishing in both scale and nature, created between Baillie and Spang. It is clear that numerous printed and edited works, as well as manuscripts, passed to and fro between these two ministers, and the highway was certainly two way. Just as Baillie, in batches between 1655 and 1658, passed via Spang the manuscript of the late Dr John Strang's *De Interpretatione et Perfectione Scripturae* to be typeset at the famous Elzevir press in Rotterdam, so printed proofs were returned to Baillie and on to Strang's surviving relatives for correction.[32] Also, when in 1645 Samuel Rutherford wished to circulate six copies of one of his pamphlets to continental divines, he sent it to Spang via Baillie, enclosing a suitable distribution list to be executed by the minister of Veere.[33] Baillie himself regularly made requests and orders to Spang for books to be supplied from the presses and bookshops of Amsterdam and Leiden, and even asked for the 'Brownist' pamphlets of those who supported the Congregationalist views of Robert Brown, minister of Midderburg. The works of many other opponents, like George Wishart and Dr Robert Forbes, along with selections of Catholic works, were also requested and

[28] Baillie, *Letters*, I, 394; *ibid.* II, 41–2; *ibid.* I, 242–3.
[29] Baillie, *Letters*, II, 181. The work referred to is *Anatomy of Independence* (1644). Keith Sprunger, *Dutch Puritanism: A History of English and Scottish Churches of the Netherlands in the Sixteenth and Seventeenth Centuries* (Leiden, 1982), 344 note.
[30] Baillie, *Letters*, III, 214. Lockyer's tract was *A Little Stone out of the Mountain: Church Order Briefly Opened* (Leith, 1652), printed by Evan Tyler; Wood's *Refutation*, (Edinburgh, 1654) was printed by Andrew Anderson.
[31] Stevenson, *King or Covenant?*, 32–5.
[32] Baillie, *Letters*, III, 256, 295, 382. Elzevir were the greatest Latin printers of the seventeenth century. Strang had been principal of Glasgow University until his enforced resignation in 1650. He died in 1654.
[33] *Ibid.* II, 275.

despatched.[34] Although Baillie and Spang were careful to carry out some of their correspondence through the 'secret wheels' of pseudonyms – Spang as 'Anderson' and Baillie as 'Jamieson'[35] – it is, nevertheless, remarkable that Baillie should have accumulated a collection of 'forbidden' literature that would have led to severe censure if found in the possession of a wayward cleric or book trader. The officers of the General Assembly who, in 1640, ransacked the Aberdeen lodgings of the late Dr Robert Baron would have been delighted at discovering such a treasure-trove.[36] Religious politics, like secular politics, was dictated by influential contacts and the tides of popularity.

Baillie's internationalism was his most remarkable characteristic. He was a rapacious reader of continental newspapers, and he received from Spang copies of the courants and mercuries of France, Brussels, Antwerp, and Amsterdam.[37] But international contacts were also of use to the Presbyterian cause, and he consistently pressed foreign divines, such as Gisbertus Voetius, Gerson Bucerus, and Willem Apollonius, and English exiles like John Paget, to write anti-episcopal, anti-congregationalist, or pro-presbyterian tracts. In general terms, they were asked to support, in an international context, the conclusions of the Solemn League and Covenant and the Westminster Assembly. With Spang's help, Baillie's Dutch campaign was very successful in the years from 1638 to 1645, and reached its peak when the classis (presbytery) of Walcheren sent official letters of support to the Westminster Assembly in 1643. The same classis then commissioned Apollonius to write a supportive Presbyterian text, *A Consideration of Certain Controversies at This Time Agitated in the Kingdom of England, Concerning the Government of the Church of God* (London, 1645), the Dutch edition of which was printed in London the year before. Also in 1645, the Synods of North Holland and South Holland passed resolutions in favour of the Presbyterian policies emanating from Westminster.[38] Yet the Reformed Church in the Low Countries was not prepared to go too far in condemnation of local Independents. The complex events of the English Civil War must have made the Dutch ponder exactly what ecclesiastical polity they were being asked to support. In a publishing sense, clarity came after the Anglo-Scottish Solemn League was signed in 1643. Between then and 1650, Baillie played a central role in publishing the liturgy of the revolution, including the *Directory of Public Worship*, first printed in Scotland in 1645 and approved by the Estates in Scotland and both English Houses of Parliament in 1644–5. Although English promises for

---

[34] Baillie, *Letters, passim*; II, 184 (Letter to Spang, 17 May 1644).

[35] *Ibid.* I, 186.

[36] J. P. Edmond, *The Aberdeen Printers, 1620–1736* (4 vols, Aberdeen,1884), IV, xxv–xxvi; James Gordon, *History of Scots Affairs* (3 vols, Aberdeen, 1841), III, 238–9.

[37] Specific titles are not mentioned in the correspondence. Baillie, *Letters*, III, 311, 324.

[38] For requests for support from 1638 to 1644 see Baillie, *Letters*, I, 110, 357; II, 75, 107, 179–80. Sprunger, *Dutch Puritanism*, 365–7.

Presbyterianism proved worthless, Baillie showed himself to be a considerable diplomat always able to counter objections with a domestic or overseas
pamphlet, or a convincing and reasoned opinion.

In spite of Baillie's involvement in Continental propaganda, both the
education of the brilliant young scholar and the awareness of the mature
controversialist depended on prevailing, domestic book supply conditions.
Balanced education and information gathering produced the personality
that despaired at clerical factionalism as the 'pulpits' of Scotland's Presbyterians 'beat [on] one another'.[39] In fact, from the 1630s to the 1660s a second
book supply phase can be identified. This was a 'new' age of theology when,
just as entertainment and practical non-fiction was beginning to develop a
readership, they were supplanted by theology and religious politics, together
with the first continuous wave of scripture printing in Scotland. Even during
the recession of the Cromwellian occupation, the publication of religious
texts remained dominant. By the 1630s and 1640s, specialist booksellers were
now well established within and without of Edinburgh, such as Andrew
Wilson, the wealthy Edinburgh bookseller and school book specialist who
operated from the 1630s to 1654, and John Neill, bookseller in Glasgow from
c. 1642 to his death in 1657.[40] The testaments of booksellers show clearly
that the network re-supplied each other throughout Scotland. A dozen or
so printers and several presses were now available in the capital, with new
presses in Aberdeen (from 1622) and Glasgow (from 1638).[41] The domestic
book trade was better prepared than ever before to handle the increased
demand created by controversy.

Yet the level of propaganda required by the Covenanter regime made it
essential to look also to the overseas press, especially to Holland. In particular, in 1639 and 1640 a variety of controversial printings was produced in
Edinburgh, London, Amsterdam, and Leiden one after the other, with Dutch
and Latin editions being printed in Holland. For example, in 1639 *The
Remonstrance of the Nobility, Barons and Burgesses* was printed by James Bryson
in Edinburgh, and also by John Canne in Amsterdam, in Dutch and English
editions. Also, in 1640 *The Intentions of the Army in Scotland* was printed by
Cloppenberg in Amsterdam, Christiaenz van der Boxe in Leiden, and Robert
Bryson in Edinburgh. This was indeed the most concerted and co-ordinated
propaganda effort in Scottish history to date. In addition, the other arm of
religious publishing, scripture, was expanding. From the 1630s to 1660s we
see a continuous wave of New Testament and Bible editions from the Scottish
press, but alongside this was a vastly increased bible supply from the presses

---

[39] Baillie, *Letters*, III, 169.

[40] For the wills and testaments of Wilson and Neill see *Bannatyne Miscellany*, II, 277–9 and NAS, Commissary
Court Records, Registers of Testaments, Glasgow, CC9/7/32 (9 September 1657).

[41] For this phase of book trade development see Mann, *The Book Trade*, 225–6. For the Glasgow and
Aberdeen presses, *ibid.* 7–33.

of Amsterdam and Leiden.[42] As a boy, Baillie had to thank the importation skills of the Presbyterian bookseller Andro Hart and his contemporaries to supply the books for his education and private library, yet in later life he depended, as author, reader, and publisher, even more on an international-ized print trade. Baillie had always wished to travel abroad extensively and finally visited Holland in 1645, his ship blown there by a fortuitous storm. He took the opportunity to visit the bookshops to acquire those books he could not purchase in Scotland or London. He was back in Holland again in 1649, visiting the young Charles II in The Hague to discuss the terms for his coronation.[43] However, the character and intellectual interests of Baillie leave us with the impression that he was throughout his life an ardent inter-nationalist and a cleric 'of the Continent'.

If Robert Baillie was master of the latest theological and international controversy, then Robert Wodrow was a veritable genius and accumulator of all manner of knowledge. Born in 1679, son of James Wodrow, professor of divinity at Glasgow, his career seemed destined to follow closely that of his father. However, after entering Glasgow University in 1691 and graduating M.A. in 1697, Robert chose the clergy rather than academia.[44] As a young man he wanted to study in Holland but never did so, and indeed he appears never to have ventured from the British Isles.

Wodrow's early published letters reveal an intensely systematic, indeed quite suffocating, approach to the gathering of information and the latest appropriate text.[45] His great work, *The History of the Sufferings of the Church of Scotland from the Restoration to the Revolution* (1721–2), is well known for its piety and pro-Presbyterian stance, while historians have barely dipped a toe in his vast manuscript collection held at the National Library of Scotland, itself a testimony to his enthusiasm for antiquarianism. Wodrow's intense interest in the lore of antiquarianism is best illustrated by his excited account of the discovery of a lost abbreviated manuscript of Calderwood's *History* in an Amsterdam bookshop in 1677. This text was then printed in 1678. In 1692 Wodrow carried out a detailed comparison with the Calderwood manu-scripts held by Glasgow University.[46] In fact, Wodrow's two literary and his-torical monuments, his own history and his collection of manuscripts, are more reflective of his energies and preoccupations before his ordination as minister of Eastwood, Paisley in 1703, after which mature contemplation and pastoral experience appear to have restrained his intellectual hunger. Yet the letters and correspondence from his twenties certainly provide a detailed

---

[42] Mann, *The Book Trade*, 80–4, 91–2, 228. For Hart see forthcoming *New DNB* article and, though somewhat dated, W. Cowan, 'Andro Hart and his press', Edinburgh Bibliographical Society Papers, I (1896), 1–15.

[43] Stevenson, *King or Covenant?*, 32.

[44] *Fasti*, v, 135–6; 'Memoirs' of Wodrow by Robert Burns, in Wodrow, *The History of the Sufferings of the Church of Scotland from the Restoration to the Revolution* [1721–2] (4 vols, Glasgow, 1828), I, ii–xviii; and Wodrow's, *Life of James Wodrow, Written by his Son* (Edinburgh, 1828), 169.

[45] L. W. Sharp (ed.), *Early Letters of Robert Wodrow, 1698–1709* (Edinburgh, 1937).

[46] Sharp, *Letters of Wodrow*, no. xx, 39–50. Letter to Archdeacon Nicholson, 3 April 1700.

and fascinating account of his catholic intellectualism and, supplying both
his private collection and the library of Glasgow University, for which he was
librarian from 1697 to 1701, his network of book agents and booksellers. Of
the first of these, there is no room here to do justice to the variety of his
chosen subjects, and the following is but a selection – history, geography,
languages, folklore, educational theory, government, geology, oriental reli-
gions, weaponry, contemporary political and religious developments, and
natural history.[47] But Wodrow's interest in natural history, often at the level
of minutiae, like the varieties of beans or the origin of mosses,[48] was accompanied by a philosophical approach that to a degree distinguishes him from
James Melville and Robert Baillie. The recording and study of natural history
provided the bridging philosophy between the salvationist fervour of the
seventeenth century and the clerical rationalism of the Enlightenment – a
journey from unquestioning spiritualism to reasoned faith and, in a scientific sense, to experimentation via observation. Wodrow, as one of the late
seventeenth and early eighteenth century *virtuosi*, was part of this linkage,
although never in an 'unholy' context. Inquiry was not a substitute for faith.[49]

Unlike Baillie, Wodrow was not a literary agent or occasional publisher,
but he did have a complex network of book trade contacts. While Spang was
essentially Baillie's 'super agent', Wodrow's network consisted of a number
of agents located in the book trade centres of Edinburgh, London, and
Leiden, although many of these individuals were, like Matthew Connell and
Matthew Simpson of the Scottish community at Leiden, former fellow students of Glasgow University. Wodrow had no reason to travel abroad himself
when so many students and contacts could be his surrogates. His Leiden
contacts acted as a clearing house for his orders from suppliers throughout
the Low Countries, with the likes of John Smith supplying books from Leers,
the Rotterdam bookseller/publisher, and Connell 'books in the catalogue'
of Van de Water, bookseller at Utrecht.[50] From Edinburgh Wodrow acquired
books and catalogues through Robert Maxwell and James Paterson, but also
had busy and intimate contacts with the Edinburgh printers David Freebairn,
John Reid, and 'Johny', his son John Reid, junior, for whom Wodrow felt
some attachment, and also the booksellers Andrew Simson and John
Vallange.[51] Sometimes the business was extremely regular, and not always
concerned with academic tomes, such as the supply by Vallange to Wodrow
of the monthly periodical *The History of the Works of the Learned*, the stream
of pamphlets from John Reid, senior, in response to the sweeping request

[47] *Ibid.* nos xxiii–xxviii for a more fulsome summary.
[48] *Ibid.* no. xxxiii, 75 (5 June 1700); no. cxxi, 236–7 (9 November 1702).
[49] David Allan, *Virtue, Learning and the Scottish Enlightenment* (Edinburgh, 1993), 9. Allan makes two essential points – first, that the Scottish Enlightenment was not irreligious, and secondly, its roots lay in post-Reformation Scotland.
[50] Sharp, *Letters of Wodrow*, no. xxi, 52 (19 February 1700); no. lxxi, 140 (24 January 1701).
[51] *Ibid.* no. xlvii, 195 (6 April 1702), for example. David Freebairn subsequently became bishop of Edinburgh.

'buy up what pamphlets [you] find', or getting the latest edition of James Watson's newspaper the *Edinburgh Gazette*, Scotland's first regular newspaper, which was published from 1699.[52] The latest and most up-to-date news was very important to this Glasgow man of letters, especially as he was remote from the capitals of both Scotland and England.

Wodrow also acquired books at the auctions of David Freebairn in Edinburgh and a 'Mr. Reid' in Glasgow.[53] Although Wodrow made gloomy remarks about Glasgow, 'much removed from . . . learned men', he also did business with the Glasgow bookbinder John Wilson, and the important stationer William Dickie, whose shop seems to have been a meeting place for the Glasgow *literati*. Curiously, in his dealings with the London trade, and somewhat in the style of Baillie, Wodrow mainly operated through the single agent James Wallace, tutor to Lord Ross, and seldom directly with his biggest London supplier, the bookseller Andrew Bell.[54] The book trade network utilized by Wodrow was undoubtedly a complex one, and this enabled him to gain valuable experience of book distribution matters, although this fell short of turning him into a real publisher. He was therefore able to advise the bookseller Andrew Simpson, via James Paterson, that the subscription for a new edition of Sedulius, the fifth-century Christian poet, would have been much larger had a prospectus been printed and circulated, though he was able to sell forty or so copies to the students of Glasgow.[55] He also wrote to the Oxford curator Edward Lhuyd in 1703, agreeing to take seven copies of his *Archaeologia Britannica* when support for the 'multi-edition' project had become essential for its survival – the first and only volume, however, did not appear until 1707.[56] Even in the thriving business of publishing, for an expanding class of *literati* some projects were stillborn.

The book supply environment in which Wodrow found himself was becoming increasingly fertile and varied. The Restoration had brought a third phase in the development of the Scottish book trade, although there was a remarkable increase and spread of 'provincial' bookselling during the late 1650s, which shows that the traditional picture of Cromwellian depression needs modification. Generally, however, building slowly from the 1660s and gathering pace by the 1670s and beyond, religious texts declined as a proportion of output and stock holding, even though the aggregate number of

---

[52] *Ibid.* no. lxxxiii, 165 (22 May 1701); no. xcvii, 196 (6 April 1702); no. cviii, 205 (8 May 1702); no. xxiii, 55 (18 May 1700).

[53] NLS, Wodrow MSS. Quarto, iii, 13; Sharp, *Letters of Wodrow*, no. lxiii, 128. Reid may be related to the Reid dynasty of Edinburgh printer/booksellers who operated from the 1670s to 1720s. See NAS, CC8/8/86 (9 April 1716) for testament of John Reid, elder.

[54] Sharp, *Letters of Wodrow*, no. xlv, 95 (24 July 1700); no. xxii, 53 (19 February 1700); no. cxxvi, 247 (14 January 1703); no. xiv, 28 (17 November, 1699). James Wallace seems to have been the tutor appointed by William, 12th Lord Ross, for his son George, the 13th Lord, who was born in 1681. See J. Balfour Paul (ed.), *The Scottish Peerage* (Edinburgh, 1904), vii, 259–62.

[55] Sharp, *Letters of Wodrow*, no. lx, 121–2 (31 October 1700).

[56] *Ibid.* no. cxxxi, 263–4 (10 September 1703). Lhuyd worked at the Ashmolean Museum.

such texts rose into the eighteenth century. What came in was a wide variety
of secular books on many aspects of science, practical non-fiction, the law,
and current affairs. By the 1680s, the domestic press was able to supply texts
of almost any genre.[57]

In addition, university, intellectual, and commercial contacts now made it
possible for the antiquarian and book-collecting Wodrow to gain supplies
from a growing number of booksellers, both specialist and general. Whereas
the first half of the seventeenth century saw the spread of Scotland's bookselling network, with booksellers supplying one another, the book merchants
of Glasgow being a particular case in point, the post-Restoration period saw
that network expand further to include ever-increasing numbers of booksellers from England, Holland, and Ireland. Religion had not disappeared as a
business interest for these traders. Indeed, the international bible trade
expanded yet again, as literally hundreds of thousands of English-language
bibles were produced for England and Scotland by the printers of Amsterdam, notably from the presses of Stam, Schippers, and Athais. Some of these
bibles were imported 'legally', and some, through Glasgow and other ports,
arrived 'illegally' in breach of the privileges of Scotland's royal printer in
Edinburgh.[58]

***

The consideration of these three giants of Scottish letters allows more general conclusions. James Melville was, in spite of his occasional role as moder-
ator to church assemblies and confessor to the Presbyterian nobility, the
more inward-looking individual, concerned for the maintaining of his own
intellectual and academic abilities, along with those of his immediate friends
and students. As a result, there is no sign of him having significant dealings
with book traders apart from Robert Lekpreuik, although he must have had
contact with 'Melvillians', supporters of his uncle, like Andro Hart and James
and Edward Cathkyn.[59] Certainly, there is no evidence of communications
with overseas book traders, and little of publishing initiative. Melville's
main preoccupation was with the fate of the Church within Scotland, and
interactions with others who were part of his uncle's religious party, and then
mostly clergymen.

Robert Baillie developed an elaborate system of contacts and correspondents
throughout Scotland, England, and Europe, although again, apart from a few
nobles and gentry, clergy and divines predominate. For Baillie, Presbyterianism

[57] For an analysis of genre see R. L. Emerson, 'Scottish cultural change 1660–1710 and the Union of 1707',
in J. Robertson (ed.), *A Union for Empire* (Cambridge, 1995), 142–3.
[58] Mann, *The Book Trade*, 92–3, 222–3, 228.
[59] For Melvillian network see Alastair J. Mann, 'Embroidery to enterprise: the role of women in the book
trade of early modern Scotland', in Elizabeth Ewan and Maureen M. Meikle (eds), *Women in Scotland, c. 1100–
c. 1750* (East Linton, 1999), 142–3.

was an international business stretching beyond the boundaries of Scottish affairs. Thus, both the divines and the book traders of the Low Countries were engaged by him directly, or through William Spang. During Baillie's years in London with the Westminster divines, from, though not continuously, 1640 to 1647, he regularly acquired books from the London theological bookseller Samuel Gellibrand. He arranged to print pamphlets with the bookseller and news printer, Nathaniel Butter, although in 1644 he expressed ironic frustration at the way the sectaries in the English Parliament used old licensing laws to slow up the printing of new Presbyterian tracts.[60] The Edinburgh press of the 1640s and 1650s he dismissed as poor and inaccurate, in spite of his initial excitement that it was up and running again in July 1638 after the hiatus caused by the Englishman and Stationers' Company man Robert Young, who departed under a cloud as printer of the hated Service Book.[61] With the exception of some modestly printed bibles and psalms, the Edinburgh press of the 1640s and 1650s was too committed to the printing of official proclamations, directives, and explanations of policy to embark on a number of publishing initiatives – politically Baillie was mostly satisfied with this, intellectually he was frustrated.

At the end of the seventeenth century, Robert Wodrow's experiences are indicative of a change in book culture for clergymen, intellectuals, and book traders. Wodrow's correspondents were not only clergymen, but those representative of an expanded intelligentsia of lawyers, academics, gentry, antiquarians, authors, literary society members, and also many book traders. Furthermore, Wodrow could look more to Edinburgh for printed news, and for a more varied and challenging publishing output. Scotland's booksellers themselves were now visiting the book capitals of the Low Countries in person rather than working only through intermediaries, such as the merchants of Leith, Bo'ness, and Glasgow. We know, for example, that the printer and bookseller Robert Freebairn, son to David Freebairn and later Jacobite printer to the Old Pretender, made at least two visits to the Netherlands, in 1702 and 1703, to purchase stock. Wodrow's concern for news of his return suggests that part of this mission was the fulfilment of a Wodrow order.[62]

But we must also ask whether the readership experiences of Melville, Baillie, and Wodrow can be perceived as a general condition for the bulk of Scotland's early modern clergy. It is certainly true that the first two of these ministers, as well as the likes of Knox, Calderwood, and Spottiswoode, came from that exceptional group of clergy who became involved in high politics as well as pastoral care. It is doubtful if Wodrow's intellectual intensity could

---

[60] Baillie, *Letters*, I, 357 (15 July 1641); H. R. Plomer (ed.) A *Dictionary of the Booksellers and Printers Who Were at Work in England, Scotland and Ireland, 1641–47* (Oxford, 1968), 81; Baillie *Letters*, I, 306 (15 March 1641); Plomer, *Dictionary*, 40–1; Baillie, *Letters*, II, 175 (3 May 1644).
[61] Baillie, *Letters*, I, 90 (22 July 1638).
[62] NLS. Wodrow MSS Quarto, II, 13. Letter Lachlan Campbell to Wodrow confirming Freebairn leaving 'Holland' with stock, 30 March 1702; Sharp, *Letters of Wodrow*, no. cxxx, 261–2 (19 April 1703).

ever be described as typical. Both the character and size of the clerical profession are in fact difficult to gauge. Taking the period from the 1580s to
1720s, it is reasonable to assume, though the number of parishes was just
over 1000, that Scotland's clergy never at any time exceeded more than 3000
men, if we include the many unemployed ousted ministers, particularly in
the 1660s and 1690s, the absent but still influential exiles in England and the
Low Countries, and those attached to the universities, along with the retired.
Many of these ministers, especially those in provincial parishes, must have
felt far removed from the centres of university study, let alone political
power. However, the number of virtually anonymous ministers recorded as
debtors in the wills of book traders confirms that the ordinary minister was
the mainstay of book demand in Scotland. This was so for book suppliers
large or small, such as the small Glasgow bookseller John Rae, who died in
1689, or John Vallange, the successful Edinburgh legal bookseller, who died
in 1712.[63] Essentially the great authors were no more important to supply
than the ordinary minister was to demand.

There was concern at all levels of the Church, from kirk sessions to the
General Assembly, that ministers should be suitably learned and educated, as
well as doctrinally sound, yet that does not mean that incumbents were
regularly found to be inadequate. Indeed, not long after the Reformation,
and at the local level, the standards expected of ministers could be very
demanding. In 1581 the Stirling presbytery could expect ministers to carry
out exercises on the interpretation of scripture with reference not only to
Calvin and Beza, but to Rudolph Gaultier of Zurich and Wolfgang Musculus
of Augsberg. The General Assembly in March 1596, in its advice against the
dangers of corruption, agreed the deprivation of those 'suche as sall be
found not given to their booke and studie of Scriptures, [or] not careful to
have bookes', and it took a similar disciplinary tone in November 1602, when
it was decided to test for a knowledge of 'the Councell of Trent, and other
writters of the controverseis of religioun' and for 'an ordinarie course of
reading the Scriptures, [and] ecclesiasticall histories', and yet there is no
particular evidence of wholesale disciplinary measures for scholarly inade-
quacy.[64] Most ministers were required to read, but also did so from a level of
education that ensured an inquisitive approach to the printed word. These
characteristics were carried over from private into public life.

Melville, Baillie, and Wodrow were extraordinary in the depth of their
learning, not merely in their interest in print culture. Their needs for private
study, knowledge, and education were not dissimilar, even though Wodrow
had more time and secure leisure to vent his enthusiasms for antiquarianism.
The three also had similar linkages with political controversy. Each had to

---

[63] NAS. cc9/7/48, 237 and cc8/8/85, 469–74.

[64] J. Kirk (ed.), *Stirling Presbytery Records, 1581–87* (SHS, 1981); Calderwood, *History*, v, 403; Peterkin, *Book of the Universal Kirk*, 427, 517–8; Melville, *Diary*, 348; Calderwood, *History*, vi, 171–2.

become intellectually and politically reconciled to the challenge to royal authority, the challenge that Buchanan justified in his great controversial text *De Jure Regni apud Scotos* (1579), the right to remove a despotic monarch.[65] Mary, Queen of Scots, Charles I, and James VII were all removed for politico-religious reasons, and the philosophical and practical implications of resistance had to be understood by all three clerics. Admittedly, Wodrow wrote his *Sufferings* after the revolution of 1688–9, looking back to write an 'accurate' and well-documented but nevertheless biased Presbyterian account. Wodrow's eighteenth-century audience was, of course, a polite one appalled at the Cameronians and other Presbyterian extremists, and so he found himself writing in his *Sufferings* an apology for the more extreme Godly who secretly he much admired.

Wodrow's sense of the past and of the Calvinism of Scotland's Protestantism was shared by Melville and Baillie. It was a journey of sacrifice for the elect and of the struggle harking back to Knox and the Reformation, but also back to a tradition of academic and clerical questioning and reformism which would have been familiar to pre-Reformation authors like the historian John Mair (1467–1550) and dramatist Sir David Lindsay (*c.* 1486–1555). Continuity is not a stranger in this age of revolutions. Indeed, what demographic historians label 'the long seventeenth century', as Scotland's population grew by about fifty per cent from 1500 to 1650 in the first dramatic rise since the thirteenth century, could be used to tag the Renaissance in Scotland. Some Renaissance developments, such as the erection of symmetrically planned municipal buildings, like Heriot's Hospital in Edinburgh (1628–59), were relatively late in European terms, even though Scotland's royal palaces of Stirling and Falkland had long before shown the architectural influences of the Renaissance.[66] University curricula catered for both the old and the new, with mathematics and science coexisting with and not usurping logic, rhetoric, the study of ancient classics, and, of course, theology. Renaissance Humanism struck a *modus vivendi* with Calvinism. In his study of neo-Stoicism in Scotland, David Allan has made a strong case for the continuity of philosophy, education, and politics throughout the sixteenth and seventeenth centuries.[67] In short, some of the great 'events', the Reformation, seventeenth-century revolutions, and Enlightenment, have encouraged historians to exaggerate the impact of change on Scottish history from the early sixteenth to early eighteenth centuries. The Scottish Renaissance may have had a short, belated head, yet it certainly showed a long, meandering

---

[65] For discussion of Buchanan's ideas on resistance and tyrannicide see J. H. Burns, *The True Law of Kingship: Concepts of Monarchy in Early Modern Scotland* (Oxford, 1996), 203–9; for a summary of ideas contained in *De Jure* see Roger Mason's 'George Buchanan, James VI and the Presbyterians', in his *Kingship and Commonweal: Political Thought in Renaissance and Reformation Scotland* (East Linton, 1998), 191–3.

[66] Miles Glendinning, Ranald MacInnes, and Aonghus MacKechnie, *A History of Scottish Architecture* (Edinburgh, 1996), 6–21, 65–8.

[67] David Allan, *Philosophy and Politics in Later Stuart Scotland: Neo-Stoicism, Culture and Ideology in an Age of Crisis, 1540–1690* (East Linton, 2000), *passim.*

tail. The continuity between Christian clerics of Protestant faith and of learned disposition was greater than might be supposed. Thus it was that Melville, Baillie, and Wodrow had many characteristics in common, not least of which were fear of God, fear of ignorance, and a hunger for the international culture of print.

University of Stirling

Index

Edmonson, Godfrey   95
education
  balanced   100
  bardic   35, 38, 47, 50–1
  books for   101
  for Catholic priesthood   22
  clergy involvement in   91
  grammar school   1–2, 93
  humanist   34, 38, 48
  and Ireland   18
  pedagogical method   3
Egerton, Sir Thomas   31–2
Elizabeth I, queen of England   1, 22,
  28, 34
Elyot, Sir Thomas   46
Elzevir press   98
Engagement crisis (1647–8)   98
Enlightenment   102, 107
  German   21
Episcopalians   98
Erasmus, Desiderius   26, 31, 37, 38,
  44, 93
ethnography   3–4, 5, 7, 11
Étienne, H.   56
Euclid   36, 47
Euripides   47
Eusebius   36
Expugnatio Hibernica   8–9, 18

Fabricius, Paulus   94
Field, Richard   95
Fisher, John, bishop   33
FitzGerald, Garret   2
FitzGerald, Maurice   12
FitzGerald, Raymond   8–9, 16
FitzStephen, Robert   12, 14, 15
Forbes, Patrick   98
Forbes, Dr Robert   98
Frederick I (Barbarossa)   37
Freebairn, David   102,
  103, 105
Freebairn, Robert   105
French Revolution   21
Fullerton, Sir James   30

Gaelic language   11
Gaidelus   7
Galloway, Patrick   92
Gaultier, Rudolph   106
Gellibrand, Samuel   105
Geneva   30
Gentili, Alberico   42
Geoffrey of Monmouth   29, 35,
  39, 43
Giraldus Cambrensis   8–9, 10, 12,
  13, 15, 16, 18
Glasgow
  book trade in   100, 103, 104,
    105, 106
  University of   92, 94, 96,
    101, 102
Goodyer, Sir Henry   32
Gresham, Sir Thomas   40
Gruffudd Gryg   39
Gruffudd Hiraethog   35
Gunpowder Plot   29, 30
Gunther of Pairis   37, 51
Guto'r Glyn   38, 39, 49
Gwyn, Robert   23, 24

Hagatius, Thaddeus   94
Harri, Master of Kidwelly   51
Hart, Andro   95, 101, 104
Harvey, Gabriel   34, 47, 48
Hecataeus of Miletus   3
Henry VII, king of England   28, 29
Henry VIII School Warwick   24
Henry II, king of England   13–15, 18
Henry, Prince of Wales   20, 30
Henryson, Robert   95
Herbert, George   25
Herodotus   3
Hippolytus   45
Historia Regum Britanniae   35
Holinshed, Raphael   2, 7
Holland   95, 99, 100, 101, 104 *see also*
  Low Countries; Netherlands
Homer   3, 36, 38, 39, 48, 49, 57,
  86, 95

Printed and bound by CPI Group (UK) Ltd, Croydon, CR0 4YY

09/06/2025

14686132-0002